James Hamilton
Arctic Watercolours

Constance Martin

Glenbow Museum, Calgary, Alberta

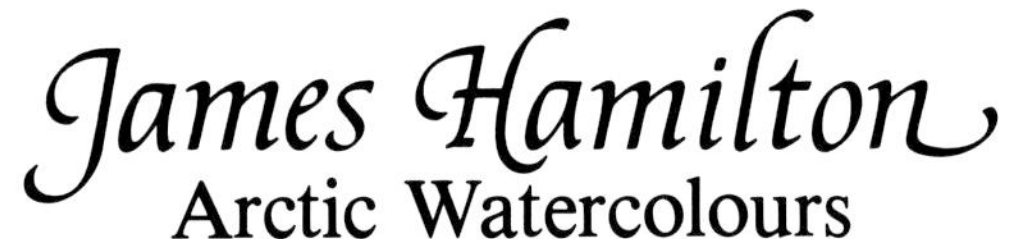

James Hamilton
Arctic Watercolours

an exhibition of arctic watercolours
organized by the Glenbow Museum,
with funding assistance from the Canada Council
and the Calgary Region Arts Foundation

October 7, 1983 — January 22, 1984

Cover:
3. James Hamilton
Ships and Kayak in Moonlight, c. 1852
watercolour
10.0 x 16.1 cm
Collection of Glenbow Museum

Contents

Foreword

Glenbow Museum proudly presents this exhibition of James Hamilton's Arctic watercolours. Drawn from the museum's Permanent Collection, they form part of a small but significant collection of oil paintings, watercolours and prints related to Arctic exploration, which once again demonstrates the diversity and richness of Glenbow's collections. These Hamilton watercolours, purchased from Kennedy Galleries in New York in 1960, have not been previously exhibited.

James Hamilton's place in nineteenth century North American landscape art has been secure, though minor, since the first retrospective exhibition of his works in this century was mounted by the Brooklyn Museum in New York in 1966. This had followed the Brooklyn's 1948 *Coast and the Sea* exhibition which featured several "forgotten" American artists, including Hamilton. John I.H. Baur's ensuing article for the Brooklyn Museum's 1951 *Bulletin* has become a basic source for all subsequent research on Hamilton. Studies on marine and landscape painting, such as John Wilmerding's extensive exhibition of the American Luminists in 1980, and Barbara Novak's important book, *Nature and Culture* of the same year, included Hamilton, but only as he relates to the better known paintings by Frederick Edwin Church, William Bradford, Alfred Bierstadt and others.

Little is published to date about Hamilton, and there is only rudimentary information available on his Arctic works. This has made the task of reconstructing the background inordinately difficult. It is for this reason that I express my admiration and appreciation for the efforts of our guest curator Constance Martin, in tracking down the information to reconstruct the facts surrounding the production of Hamilton's Arctic watercolours and their relationship to the subsequent engravings.

Using the works by Hamilton at Glenbow as a base, Mrs. Martin has sought works and information across North America. The result of these efforts is the first exhibition to focus on Hamilton's Arctic images. Our understanding and appreciation of Hamilton's paintings is increased by the inclusion of works by Elisha Kent Kane, which clearly show the different approaches used by the two artists: the significant contrast of Hamilton's romantic interpretation from the more factual on-the-spot watercolours produced by Kane. The research for this exhibition has increased our knowledge of Hamilton and will form a sound basis for future work on the artist.

The Glenbow Museum gratefully acknowledges the funding assistance of the Canada Council and the Calgary Region Arts Foundation in the preparation of this exhibition and publication.

Patricia Ainslie
Acting Curator of Art
Glenbow Museum

Acknowledgements

When Mr. Duncan Cameron, director of the Glenbow Museum, informally suggested, after learning of my interest in Arctic imagery, that I look at the James Hamilton Arctic watercolours in the Museum's collection, I was very pleased. From this beginning and with the encouragement of Dr. Jeremy Adamson, former curator of art, Glenbow Museum, and a recognized scholar of North American landscape painting, I found to my pleasure the opportunity to be the guest curator of this exhibition. I am grateful for that opportunity and the guidance and support I have had from the Glenbow's staff in the preparation of both the exhibit and the catalogue. In particular I would like to thank the following individuals: Barbara Tyler and Patricia Ainslie for their patient and skillful administration; Jane Poole for the imaginative design and production of the catalogue; Marion DeVries, Joyce Law, Kevin Oke, Pamela Smith, Eva Smithwick, Maeve Spain, Vincent Varga, Gary Tucker, Terry Hagan and Patricia Olynyk for the thoughtful assistance of various kinds.

My attempt to place the James Hamilton watercolours in their historical and art historical context would have been far more difficult without the following individuals and institutions who lent so generously from their own collections: Mrs. W. Beyer Africa; Mrs. Florence Johnson; Mrs. Robert Grinnell; Dr. Thomas Kane; Mr. Gary Trinetti; Mr. Ian McKibbin White; The Library Company, Philadelphia; The American Philosophical Society, Philadelphia; Seneca Falls Historical Society, New York; and the Metropolitan Toronto Library.

To the following archives, libraries, galleries and individuals who helped with the research I would like to express my gratitude: Miss Linda Ferber of the Brooklyn Museum; Mr. Lawrence Fleischman of Kennedy Galleries, New York; Dr. William Gertz of City University of New York; Dr. Chauncey Loomis of Dartmouth College; Dr. Frank Paddock, Lenox, Massachusetts; Mrs. Lisa Palmer, New York; Dr. Henry Phelps; Ms. Angela Saunders of the Silverman Gallery, Alexandria, Virginia; Mrs. Jean Tener and Mrs. Apollonia Steele of the Special Collections, University of Calgary Library; Mr. Jerry Thompson of the Arctic Institute of North America, Calgary; Miss Alison Wilson of the Polar Archives, Washington, D.C.; Mr. John Wilmerding of the National Gallery, Washington, D.C.; Miss Helen Sanger of the Frick Art Reference Library, New York; the New York Historical Society; the New York Public Library; the Peabody Museum, Salem, Massachusetts; the Pennsylvania Academy of the Fine Arts, and the Philadelphia Historical Society.

In addition I wish to mention the valuable information concerning the Kane and Grinnell families I learned from Mrs. W. Beyer Africa, great-niece of Elisha Kent Kane, and Mr. Alexander Grinnell.

Although he was not directly involved with this project I would nevertheless like to express my appreciation to Dr. Anthony Rasporich of the University of Calgary, whose insightful supervision saw my masters thesis to completion, which in turn provided the inspiration for this study. Finally my special thanks to Dr. Jeremy Adamson for his knowledgeable advice and the great care he gave to the reading and editing of the catalogue manuscript.

Constance Martin
Guest Curator
Glenbow Museum

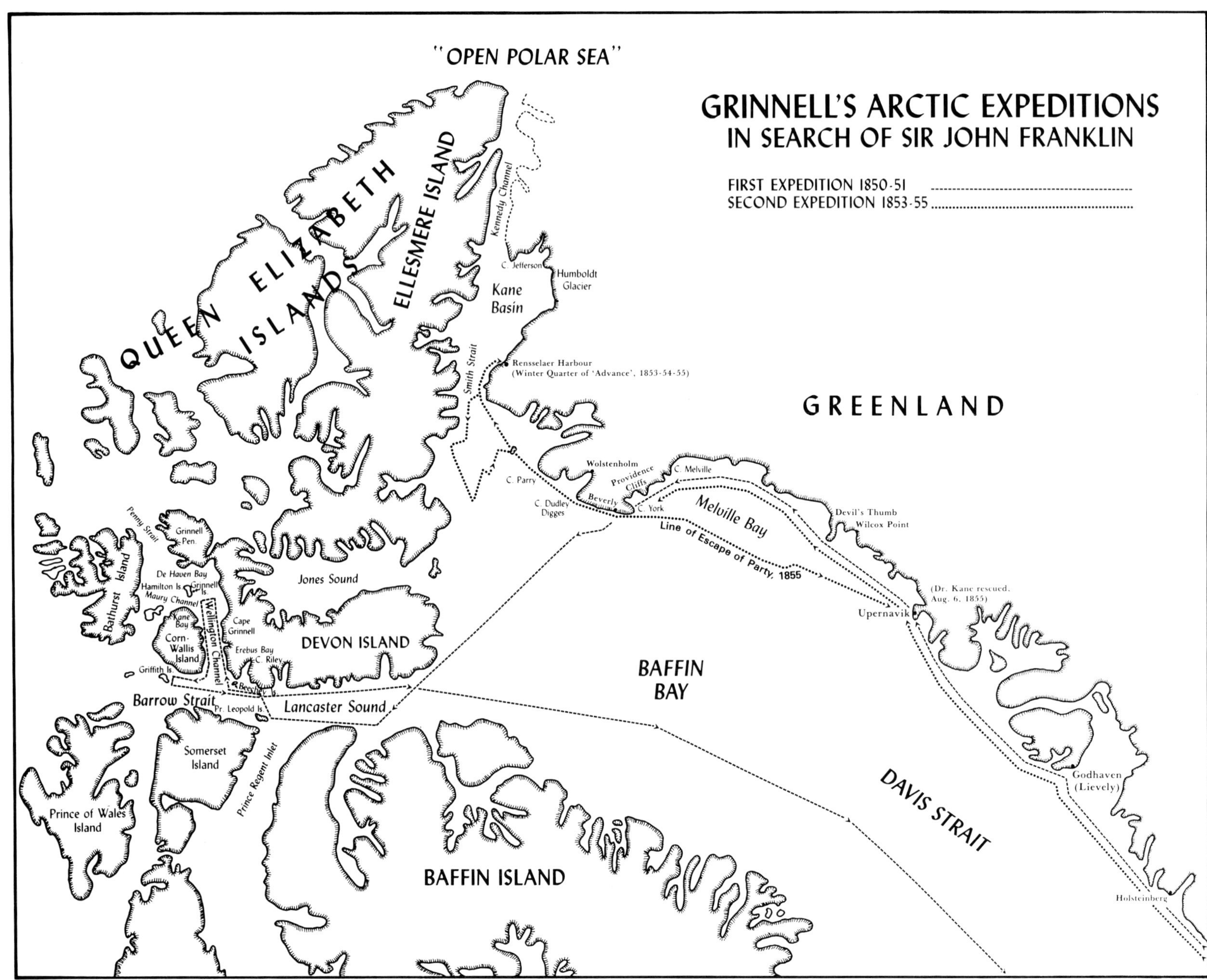

"OPEN POLAR SEA"
GRINNELL'S ARCTIC EXPEDITIONS
IN SEARCH OF SIR JOHN FRANKLIN
FIRST EXPEDITION 1850-51
SECOND EXPEDITION 1853-55
QUEEN ELIZABETH ISLANDS
ELLESMERE ISLAND
Kennedy Channel
C. Jefferson
Humboldt Glacier
Kane Basin
Smith Strait
Rensselaer Harbour
(Winter Quarter of 'Advance', 1853-54-55)
GREENLAND
Wolstenholm
Providence Cliffs
C. Melville
C. Parry
Beverly
C. Dudley Digges
C. York
Melville Bay
Devil's Thumb
Wilcox Point
Line of Escape of Party, 1855
Penny Strait
Grinnell Pen.
De Haven Bay
Hamilton Is.
Grinnell Is.
Maury Channel
Jones Sound
Bathurst Island
Kane Bay
Corn-Wallis Island
Wellington Channel
Cape Grinnell
Erebus Bay
C. Riley
Griffith Is.
Beechey
DEVON ISLAND
(Dr. Kane rescued,
Aug. 6, 1855)
Upernavik
Barrow Strait
Pr. Leopold Is.
Lancaster Sound
BAFFIN BAY
Somerset Island
Prince Regent Inlet
DAVIS STRAIT
Godhaven (Lively)
Prince of Wales Island
BAFFIN ISLAND
Holsteinberg

James Hamilton
Arctic Watercolours

I

I try in vain to be persuaded that the pole is the seat of frost and desolation; it ever presents itself to my imagination as the region of beauty and delight. There . . . the sun is forever visible; its broad disk just skirting the horizon, and diffusing a perpetual splendour . . . there snow and frost are banished; and sailing over a calm sea, we may be wafted to a land surpassing in wonders and in beauty every region hitherto discovered on the habitable globe.

Frankenstein, Mary Shelley, 1818[1]

The above quotation reveals a human longing for an earthly paradise that in the nineteenth century often found its expression in the romantic imagery of landscape painting. Arctic explorers, searching for the elusive Northwest Passage or the imaginary Open Polar Sea, sought solace in this dream in which science and romance were inexorably intertwined.

The twenty-one Arctic watercolours by the artist James Hamilton (1819-1878) at the Glenbow Museum, which form the nucleus of this exhibition, provide a rich contemporary study of romantic imagery in polar landscapes. These paintings were among the many Hamilton prepared as models for the woodcuts and engravings illustrating the journals of American polar explorer Elisha Kent Kane (1820-1857). The watercolours themselves were based on Kane's own precise on-the-spot sketches in the far north.

The idea of engraved views of Arctic scenes was not new. In the second half of the eighteenth century, illustrations of unknown lands became an integral part of travel literature. In the nineteenth century, each of Britain's expeditions in search of the Northwest Passage was followed by a handsomely illustrated narrative of the journey. Although the images were meant to record nature objectively, they also closely reflected current aesthetic conventions of the time, conventions which were rooted in neoclassicism and romantic ideas of the sublime and the picturesque.[2]

Enhanced by James Hamilton's illustrations, Kane's publications, *The U.S. Grinnell Expedition in Search of Sir John Franklin, 1850-51*, (1854) and *Arctic Explorations: The Second Grinnell Expedition in Search of Sir John Franklin, 1853, '54, '55*, (1856) received popular and wide acclaim. The most immediate precedent for the imagery was undoubtedly a folio edition of lithographs of Arctic scenes by the British explorer-artist Lieutenant William Browne (see illustration). These lithographs commemorated the first voyage in search of Franklin in 1848-49, and Kane had examined the folio before his departure with the U.S. Grinnell expedition in 1850.[3]

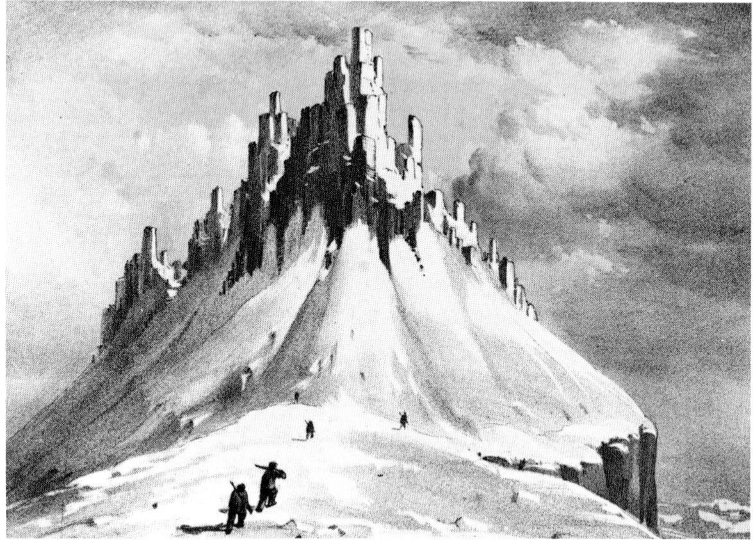

1. William Browne
Termination of Cliffs Near Whaler Point, Port Leopold, c. 1849
lithograph
37.5 x 27.5 cm sheet
Collection of Glenbow Museum

Kane was a world traveller before his famed polar voyages. By 1850, he had already journeyed to South America, Africa, Europe, and the Far East. Born into a distinguished Philadelphia family and well educated, he became a Naval medical doctor. Though Kane was small of stature and physically frail as the result of a rheumatic heart condition, he sought out challenges of physical endurance, and thus enthusiastically joined the arduous U.S. Grinnell expedition to the Arctic in 1850 as ship's surgeon and again in 1853 as leader. Moreover, he was a learned man with broad scientific interests. According to the present day author-explorer, C.C. Loomis, Kane was a man who felt at home in chemistry, physics, geology, and zoology; and, one who observed, measured, and noted all natural phenomena almost by reflex action.

American whalers had long travelled to the polar regions, but the serious search for a Northwest Passage had been a predominantly British enterprise from the first quarter of the nineteenth century. When Sir John Franklin's expedition of 1845 did not return, international attention was focused on the drama. Repeated newspaper reports and the new picture magazines such as the *Illustrated London News* aroused widespread interest in Franklin's mysterious fate. At the same time that Lady Jane Franklin appealed directly to President Zachary Taylor of the United States, a wealthy New York shipbuilder, Henry Grinnell became concerned over the lost expedition and offered to sponsor a voyage in search of Franklin. After some hesitation Congress agreed to a co-sponsorship of Grinnell's expeditionary search of 1850 and again later, the second search in 1853.

Aside from the humanitarian effort to help find the missing Franklin and his crew of 135 men, scientific questions about the Arctic intrigued American oceanographers and further stimulated their interest. As absurd as it seems today, the U.S. Navy based its sailing instructions to the Grinnell expeditions on the notion that beyond a barrier of ice ringing the northern shores of the globe lay a warm water sea. This age-old romantic belief had attracted the imagination of seafarers and geographers for centuries. Poetically related to visions of an earthly paradise in the New World, it had been an important stimulus to Britain's search for the Northwest Passage. Direct experience in the impenetrable ice-choked seas, however, had dampened the dream. Nevertheless, the idea of a mediterranean sea capping the globe continued to be a focus of scientific discussion late into the nineteenth century.[5]

In the end, the goals of the two American voyages were not realized: Franklin was not found, and the Open Polar Sea proved to be an illusion. The apparent failure of the U.S. Grinnell expeditions, however, did not negate the explorers' important accomplishments: the 1850-51 voyage's discovery of Grinnell Island in Wellington Channel and the 1853-55 expedition's mapping of the narrow passage between Ellesmere Island and the east coast of Greenland to latitude 80° 58'.[6] Locked in the Arctic ice for two and a half years, Kane's expedition of 1853-55 learned much about survival from the indigenous Eskimos. This contact left a legacy of good relations, and later expeditions were received with kindness and generosity.[7]

The first voyage of 1850-51 attempted a passage through Lancaster Sound and north into Wellington Channel with the intent of penetrating the Arctic ice into open water. The attempt was unsuccessful and in 1853-55, with Kane as commander, the second U.S. Grinnell expedition sailed up the west coast of Greenland as far as latitude 78°. Here Kane's ship, the 'Advance', was icebound. Further progress by sled and on foot by two of Kane's crew reached latitude 81° 22', "...the northernmost land ever trodden by a white man," where the explorers saw "open water stretching to the northern horizon. The unending shore line was washed by shining waters without a sign of ice."[8] Kane believed it was the scientific culmination of their journey, and declared, "The great North Sea, the Polynia has been reached..."[9]

Not until our own century, however, was it demonstrated that what the men witnessed was a transitory phenomenon, formed by local currents of wind and water.[10] Nevertheless, the story of Kane's adventures, especially his party's extraordinary escape south in 1855 — covering 1300 miles by sled and small boat after the abandonment of their ice-locked ship — made Kane a world-renowned hero.

At home in Philadelphia in 1856, however, Kane faced considerable pressure from his publishers. For both expeditions, the explorer's reluctant intentions had been to write popular, rather than scientific books. Kane wrote, "It is a sacrifice,"[11] but he hoped to counteract this later with learned works of his scientific findings from each expedition. In the meantime, he continued, "My wish is to make a centre-table book, fit as well for the eyes of children as of refined women."[12] Ironically, the strain of writing elicited more complaints from the determined explorer than did his years in the Arctic. In letters to his Philadelphia publisher, Childs and Peterson, Kane lamented, "the wretched book...has been my coffin."[13] Such was not far from the truth: the author; his frail health broken, died in 1857.

II

For James Hamilton, the commission to illustrate the Kane Arctic narratives was perfectly suited to his talents. Born in Ireland in 1819, the artist emigrated to Philadelphia, Kane's home, at the age of fifteen. A few years later, encouraged by John Sartain (1808-1897), the well-known Philadelphia engraver, who was to collaborate with him much later on the first Kane publication, Hamilton undertook drawing lessons. Watercolour instruction must have soon followed, for as Sartain wrote, "...at the commencement of his career he devoted himself exclusively to that branch of art."[14]

We do not know who his local teachers were, but artists' manuals in the 1840's were widespread. Among these were several by the English artist, Samuel Prout (1783-1852). Hamilton must have known Prout's works, for in 1840 he included an oil painting, *View of Venice after Prout*[15] in an exhibition for the Philadelphia Artists Fund Society. Prout advocated the importance of imagination in landscape art through a broad and simple style , and a loose freedom and breadth of effect. Prout's manuals were designed as "an antidote to the feeble fidgetty performance of laborious artists."[16] Complementary to Prout's technique was Hamilton's interest in the English method of watercolour, a method in which broad transparent washes rather than tightly delineated details were essential. It seems in fact that Hamilton was one of the first in America to employ this painterly mode.[17]

By 1850, Hamilton was an established marine painter who had exhibited regularly at the Pennsylvania Academy of the Fine Arts for a decade. The artist's distinctive, loosely painted landscapes and marine subjects were earning him by the 1850's the sobriquet of "the American Turner."[18] Hamilton may have encountered some of the English painter's works at an exhibition of 400 British watercolours in Boston in 1840,[19] or he may not have seen the British landscapists work until his first trip to England in 1854.[20] However, Turner was known in North America by the 1840's, primarily through his engraved compositions, and to Hamilton like many of his contemporaries the grandeur of his style was a revelation. Hamilton became "...a most devoted admirer and student ...dwelling long and earnestly on models of such superlative excellence."[21]

James Hamilton's most important teacher, however, was nature itself. Emily Sartain, the engraver's niece, wrote that, instead of undertaking much copy-work, the young visionary sought the woods, the mountains, and the sea, for his models.[22] It was here that Hamilton's sensitivity to "motion and force, the roll of thunder clouds, the play of lightning, the confused rush of the maker,"[23] set him apart from the so-called realistic school, which concentrated on tightly constructed compositions of carefully delineated details.

A critic in the New York *Herald Tribune* in 1866 described Hamilton as one who threw realism overboard, with all the strength

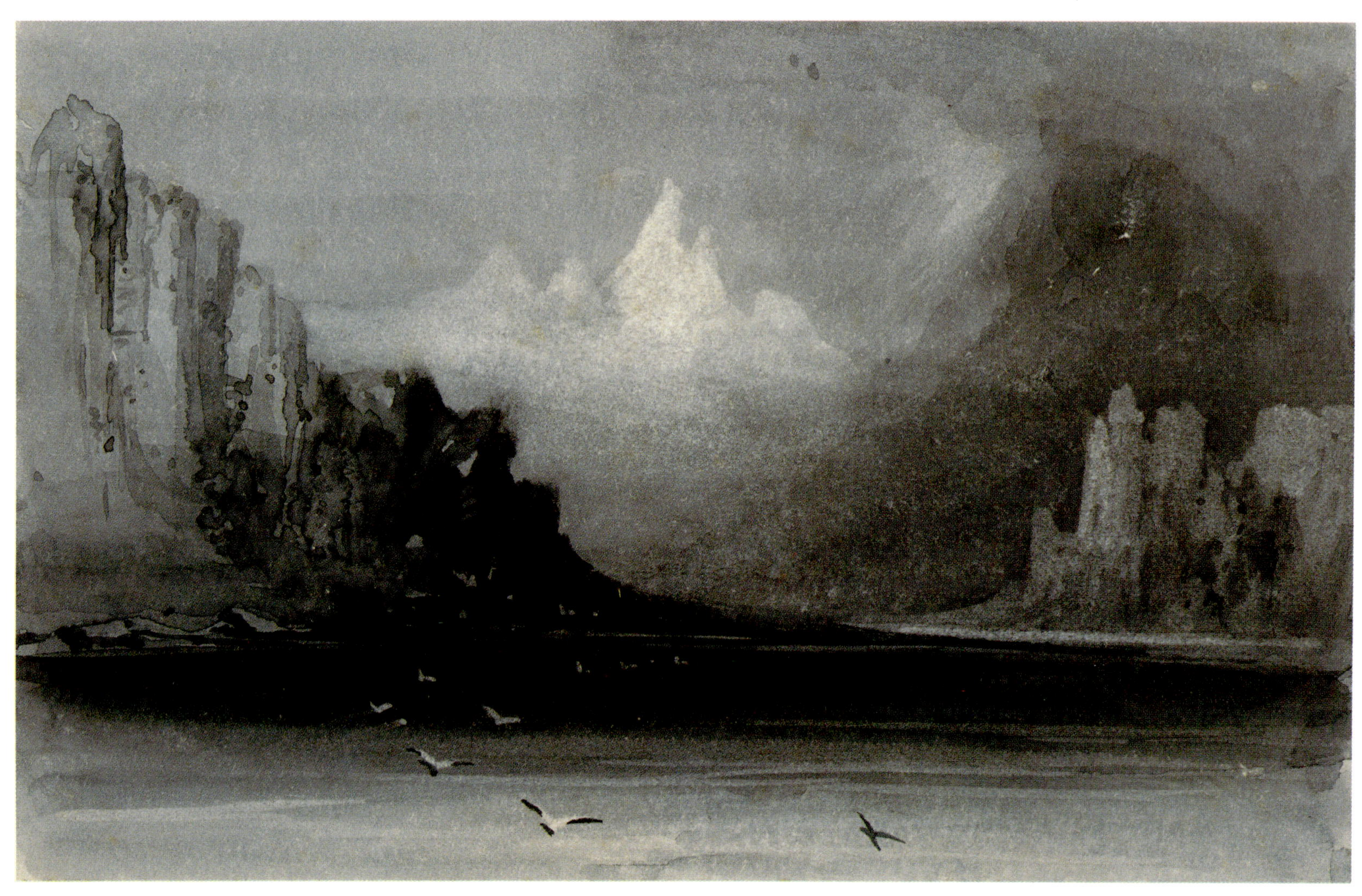

32. James Hamilton
Greenland Fiord, n.d.
watercolour
10.5 x 16.7 cm
Collection of Glenbow Museum

there was in him, scorning it utterly. This placed him, the critic said, in the new school by the same logic that put Turner there, that made Turner the great modern head of the school. The writer, like John Sartain a decade earlier and Emily Sartain in the 1870s, concluded, however, that Hamilton was not an imitator of Turner, for not only did Turner have a far greater range, but his sense of "truth to nature" had a different emphasis. Hamilton was a distinctly American painter, clearly nationalistic in his style and in his approach. According to the critic, if he could be called the "American Turner" then it was doubted that he was "American anything."[24]

A practical reason for Hamilton painting in watercolour was that this was the preparatory medium from which engravings, woodcuts or lithographs were made. Book and magazine illustration was a growing field and an important aspect of Hamilton's career. Prior to the Kane project, he illustrated John Frost's *The Pictorial History of the American Navy* (1845) and provided compositions for *Godey's Magazine and Lady's Book*. Also in this genre are Hamilton's many designs inspired by the literature of Charles Dickens, James Fenimore Cooper, Samuel Coleridge, Samuel Rogers and William Shakespeare.

As for Hamilton's oil paintings, they too, like Turner's, reflect his early watercolour training: indeed for many years it had been the ambition of landscape painters to imitate in oils the effects of the watercolour school.[25] Two marine compositions in oil, *The Vision of Columbus* (1850) (as illustrated in the Brooklyn Museum catalogue, *James Hamilton*, page 33), prophetic of Kane's expedition, and *One of the Ships of the Grinnell Expedition* (circa 1852) both have the fluid, painterly quality that is the hallmark of the Arctic watercolours.

III

Exactly why Kane chose Hamilton as his illustrator is unknown. Certainly, Hamilton's romantic pictorial style with its emphasis on sweeping grandeur was well suited to the intentions of Kane and his publisher to produce a popular, centre-table book. There is an indication that Kane may have had Hamilton in mind before the first expedition even returned in 1851. In a passage from his personal diary which appears in the published 1853 narrative, Kane wrote: "Let me make a picture for you without a jot of fancy about it and you [Kane's brother] get 'H' to put it into colours if

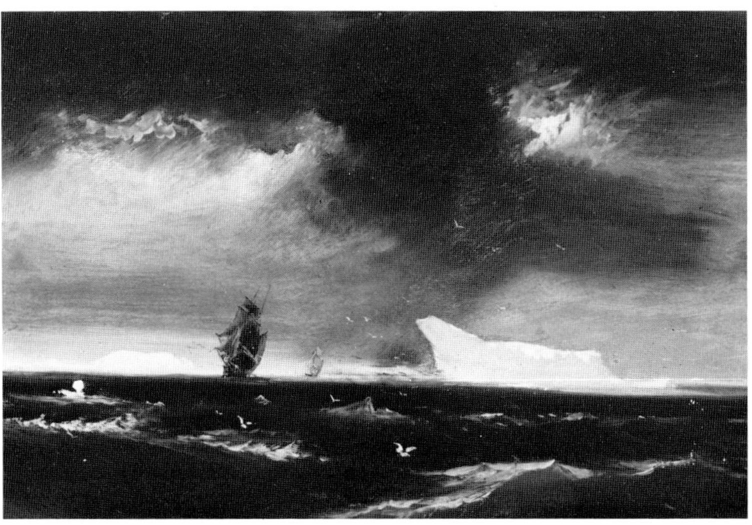

2. James Hamilton
One of the Ships of the Grinnell Expedition, c. 1852
oil on wood
29.3 x 44.5 cm (sight)
Collection of Mrs. Robert S. Grinnell, New York

you can."[26]

To facilitate his interpretive rendering of the hundreds of illustrative instances in Kane's well-filled folios, Hamilton moved into Kane's home and "for more than a month . . . occupied the doctor's [Kane's] room, that night and day might be given to their execution."[27]

Hamilton had great respect for Kane's own artistic skills. After the explorer's death, he wrote to William Elder, Kane's biographer: "Every fragment is jotted down with a perception and feeling which seize the special character of the minutest particle defined and yet its minutia in no way conflicting with the grandeur of the subject."[28] The accuracy of this description can be seen in examples of Kane's own work. *Upper Island Baffin, July 12, 1851*, precisely delineated in pencil and watercolour, suggests he may have had draftsman's training in the Navy. A comparison of Kane's *Upper Island Baffin* and Hamilton's *Securing the Brig* reveals, without detracting from either, the difference between their two styles.

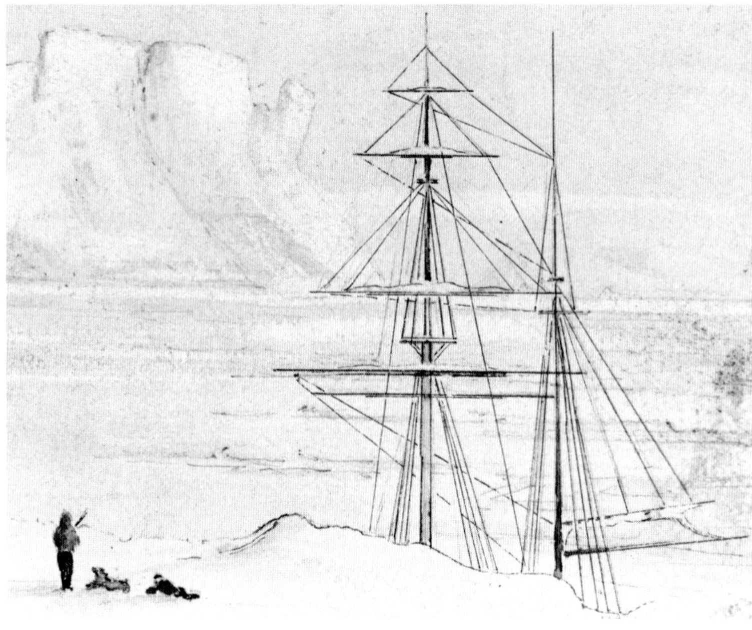

31. Elisha Kent Kane
Upper Island, Baffin, July 12, 1851, 1851, detail
watercolour, pencil and ink
12.2 x 24.7 cm
Collection of Mr. Gary Trinetti, Kane, Pa.

27. James Hamilton
Securing the Brig, n.d., detail
watercolour
19.9 x 29.3 cm
Collection of Mr. Gary Trinetti, Kane, Pa.

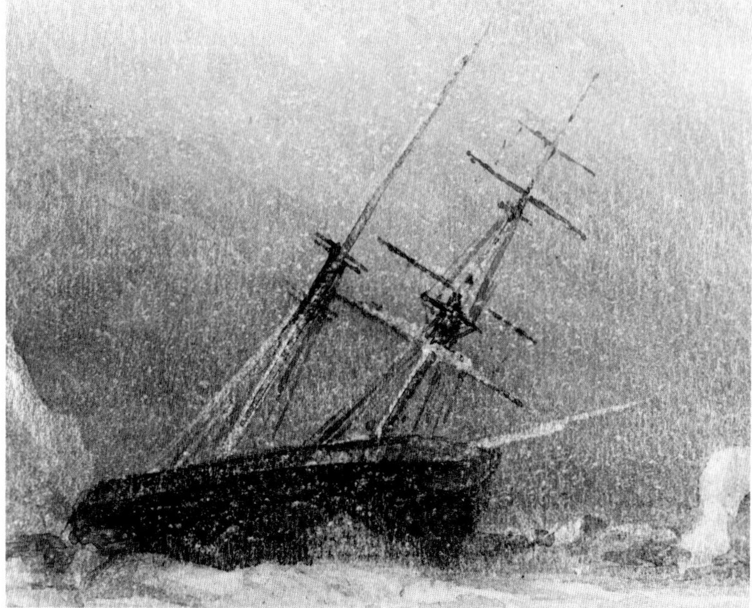

IV

The Arctic watercolours included in this exhibition are only a small number of those Hamilton prepared for Kane's two books. Although the subjects are identifiable from the explorer's text, not all were actually included in Kane's books. Icebergs, glaciers, vast spaces, turbulent seas and skies, warm glowing light, refracted light and the Beechey Island graves found at Franklin's first winter quarters form the dominant subjects of the Arctic scenes. All evoke the sensibility of the natural sublime, particularly the strange, majestic strength of nature and the sense of human fragility set against such awesome splendour.

Depictions of icebergs in particular provoked flights of fancy, described by Kane in his narrative as of ineffable beauty and mystery:

> Certain it is that no objects ever impressed me more. There was something about them so slumberous and so pure, so massive yet so evanescent, so majestic in their cheerless beauty, without, after all, any of the salient points which give character to description, that they almost seemed to me the material for a dream, rather than things to be definitely painted in words. [29]

In the small pen-and-ink wash, *Entering Lancaster Sound*, the gigantic architectural form of an iceberg dwarfs the tiny man-made ship. In another watercolour, *Melville Bay*, the two vessels of the 1850 voyage, 'Rescue' and 'Advance', are locked in the ice. Boats and men are surrounded by mountainous structures of a neo-Gothic magnificence and are reduced to the infinitesimal.

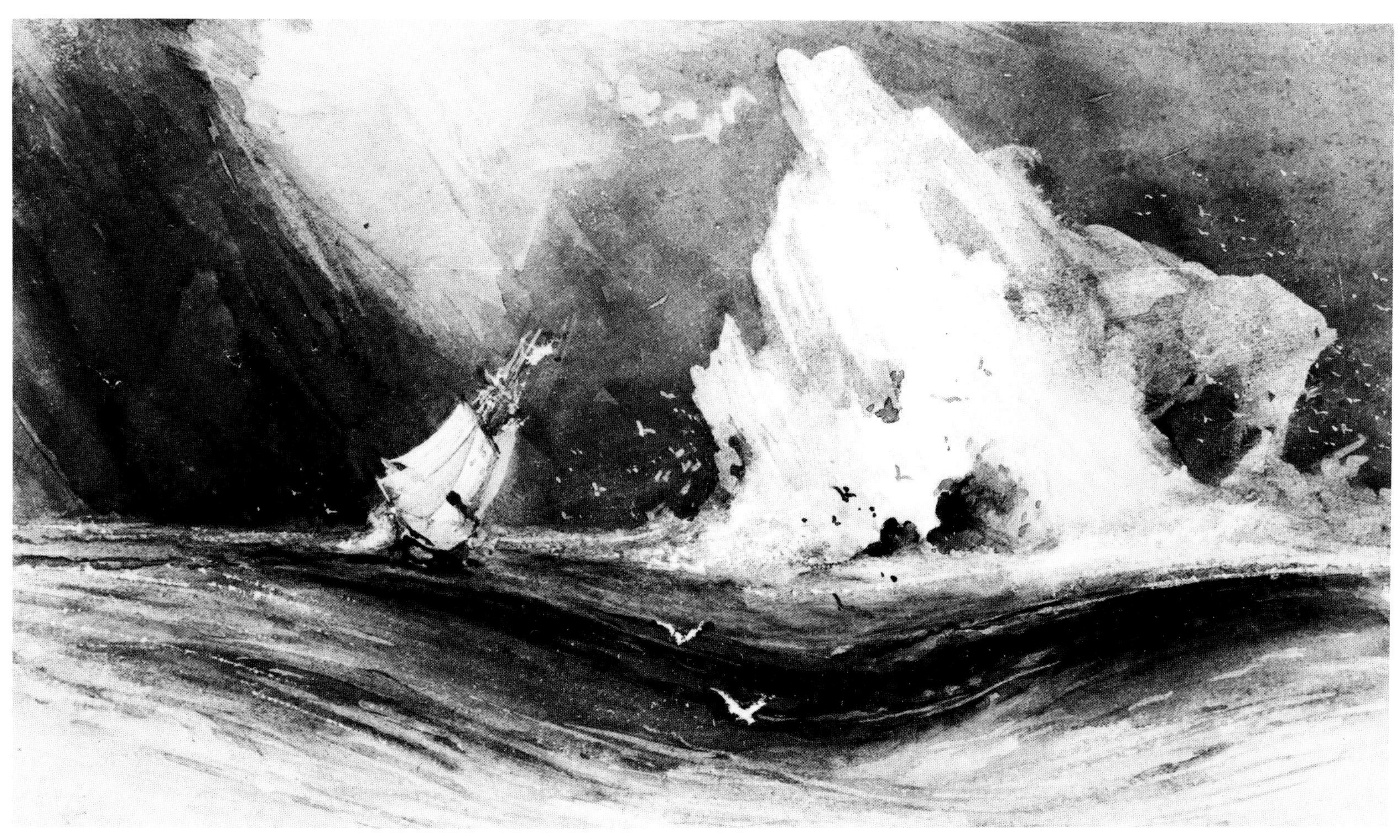

19. James Hamilton
Entering Lancaster Sound, 1850, c. 1852
ink wash and white highlights
10.7 x 18.2 cm
Collection of Mr. Gary Trinetti, Kane, Pa.

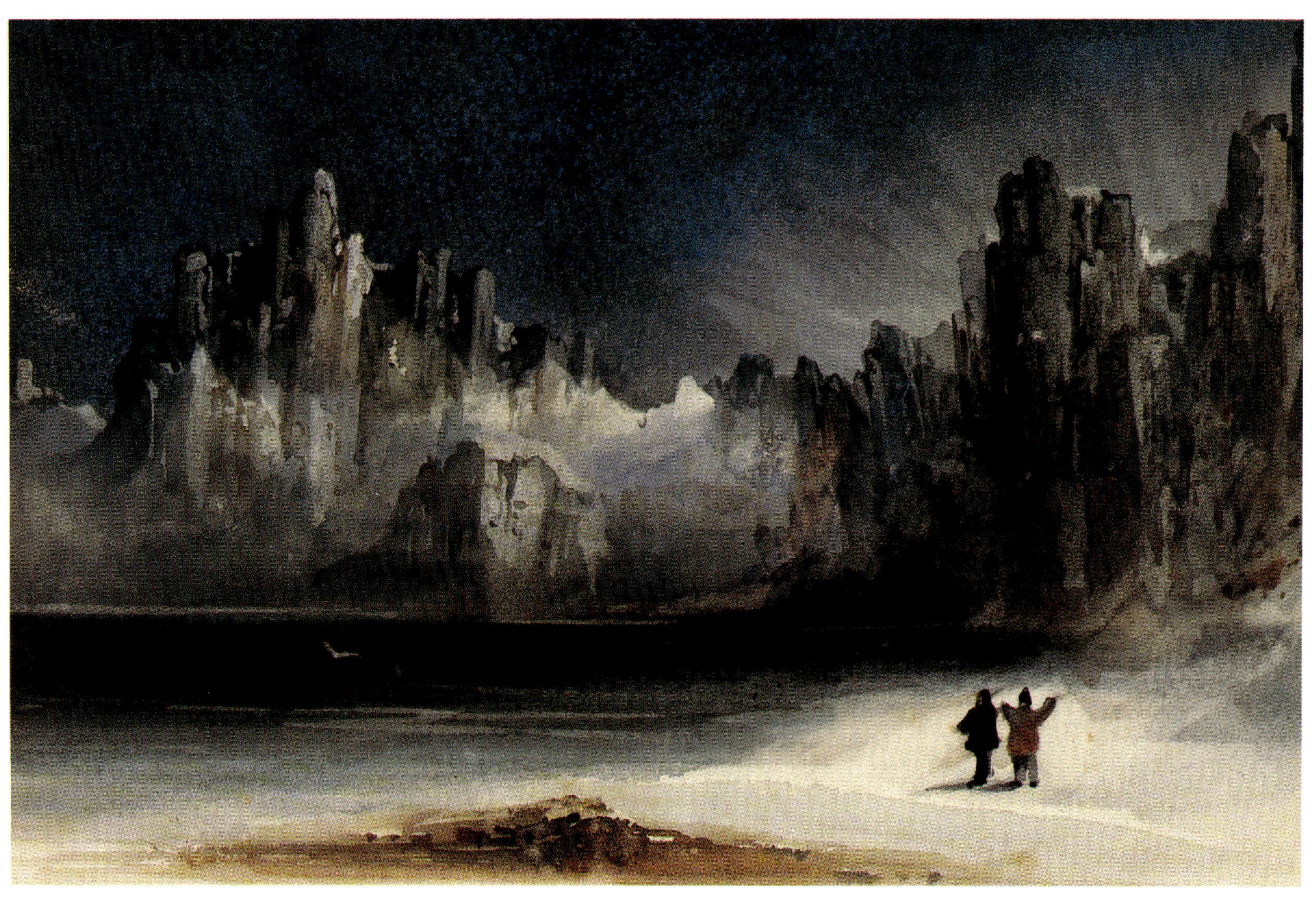

34. James Hamilton
Greenland Fiord, n.d.
watercolour
16.0 x 24.3 cm
Collection of Glenbow Museum

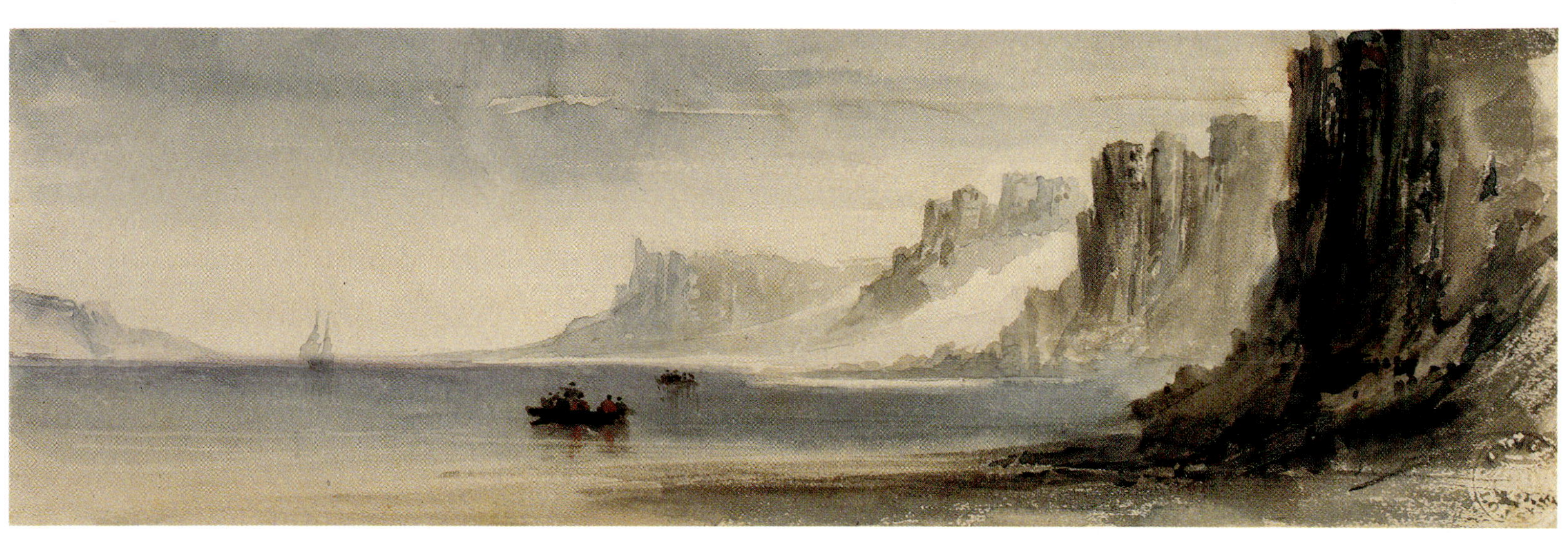

23. James Hamilton
   Wellington Channel, Beechey Island, c. 1852
   watercolour over pencil
   9.5 x 30.1 cm
   Collection of Glenbow Museum

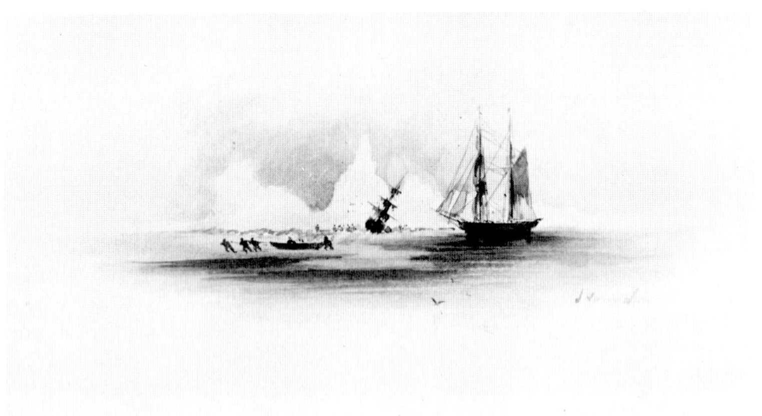

13. James Hamilton
Melville Bay, n.d.
watercolour
16.9 x 27 cm sheet
Collection of Glenbow Museum

Melville Bay, an indentation of about 150 miles on the west coast of Greenland, is a treacherous region. Hundreds of icebergs are formed from its glaciers and move into the adjacent waters of Baffin Bay. Nicknamed "Devil's Nip" or "Bergie Hole", Melville Bay was the graveyard for over 210 ships destroyed by ice between 1819 and 1850. [30]

Hamilton's *Melville Bay* watercolour, which he painted from Kane's on-the-spot sketches, became the inspiration for a subsequent oil painting, *Breaking Up of an Iceberg in Melville Bay.* A curving sea formation (found also in the watercolour *Entering Lancaster Sound*) establishes the foreground for a fairytale scene of awesome wonder: ice tumbles from the pinnacled structure, and men break and push huge floes while sea birds and deep green water allude to an abundance of life. Enveloped by light, the scene, in spite of its dangers, depicts a land of riches and glittering ice castles. As magical architectural structures, icebergs were a principal focus for Hamilton.

Equal in their power to evoke the sublime are the artist's images of the eastern Arctic's dramatic fiords, glacial masses, and towering cliffs. In *Greenland Fiord,* the massive pinnacles of rock form an impenetrable fortress surrounding a calm, restful bay. In the foreground, small figures gaze reverently at the glacial wilderness and gesture in response to the wonders they behold. Two other compositions, *Wellington Channel* and *Erebus Bay, Yellow*

Sunset contrast impervious rock with peaceful waters and distant horizons bathed in warm light, evoking a sense of supernatural protection. Even more explicit of a spiritual presence are the parting clouds in *Ships and Kayak in Moonlight,* in which two vessels reminiscent of *The Vision of Columbus* sail resolutely north.

Ice, not for its structural form, but for its strange unpredictable properties, is the subject of *'Rescue' Nipped,* and *'Rescue' in Her Arctic Ice Dock.* The latter painting became the inspiration for Hamilton's most ambitious oil painting of the Arctic, known by the same title. In *'Rescue' Nipped,* the exaggerated tilt of the ship locked in the ice suggests the possibility of imminent destruction. In the second painting, Kane's expedition has turned the unusual properties of ice to their advantage in creating an Arctic ice dock from which to effect repairs to the ship's keel. The endless space of the surrounding scene enveloped in an haze reminds the viewer of the small group's vulnerability. Kane wrote: "It is a landscape such as Milton or Dante might imagine...inorganic, desolate, mysterious." [31]

Less terrifying, yet more evocative, is the atmospheric condition known as refraction. A mirage created under certain conditions, refraction causes illusive forms to be thrown above and below the horizon line. In his narrative, calling the experience "phantasmagoric," Kane wrote that it was beyond his powers of description. [32] Sometimes an object like a ship would be reflected in the sky in reverse as many as three times.

In one of the several watercolours Hamilton rendered of this hallucinatory effect, *Refraction* presents ghostly ships mirrored in the sky, surrounded by unearthly shapes in a purple haze. An ideal subject to reveal the artist's brilliant watercolour technique and poetic tendencies, the image unfortunately suffered considerably when turned into a woodcut for the book illustration.

Important historically and symbolically are the watercolours of Beechey Island. Three graves discovered here in the summer of 1850 mark Franklin's first winter quarters. The small tombstones beneath the towering cliffs became a well-known Arctic landmark. Three of Hamilton's paintings record this historic scene. *Cape Riley, Erebus Bay, August 27, 1850* commemorates the day the graves were found by the American and British explorers. It was a day of hope, for it was believed that the discovery would soon lead to finding Franklin. [33] *Erebus Bay, Yellow Sunset,* mentioned earlier, conveys the same optimism through its golden colour. In *Beechey Island Graves,* the mood is ironic, for the landscape, now clouded by fog and mist, becomes a reminder of the never-solved mystery.

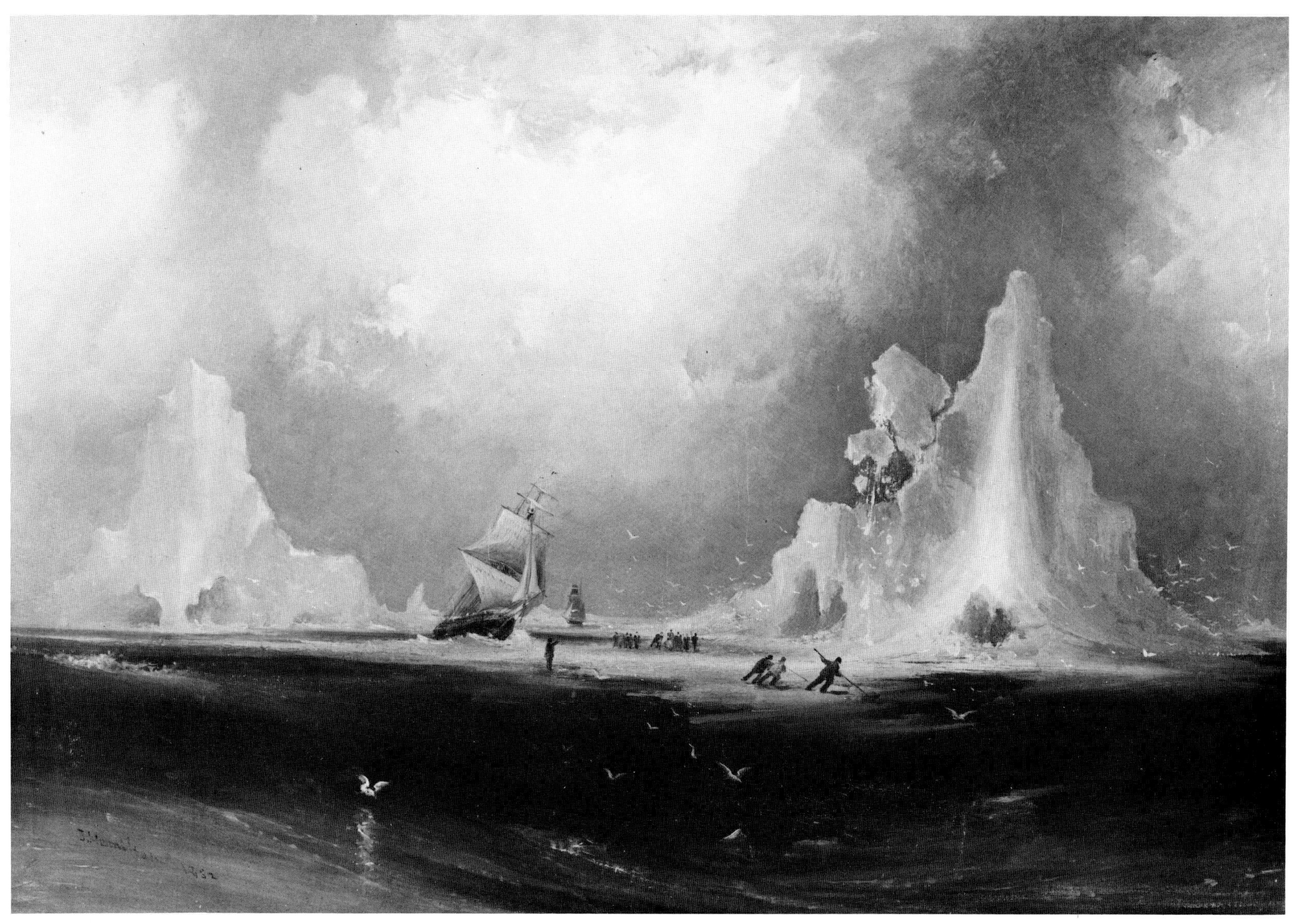

35. James Hamilton
Breaking up of An Iceberg in Melville Bay, 1852
oil on canvas
62.3 x 91.4 cm
Collection of Mr. Ian McKibbon White, San Raffael, Ca.

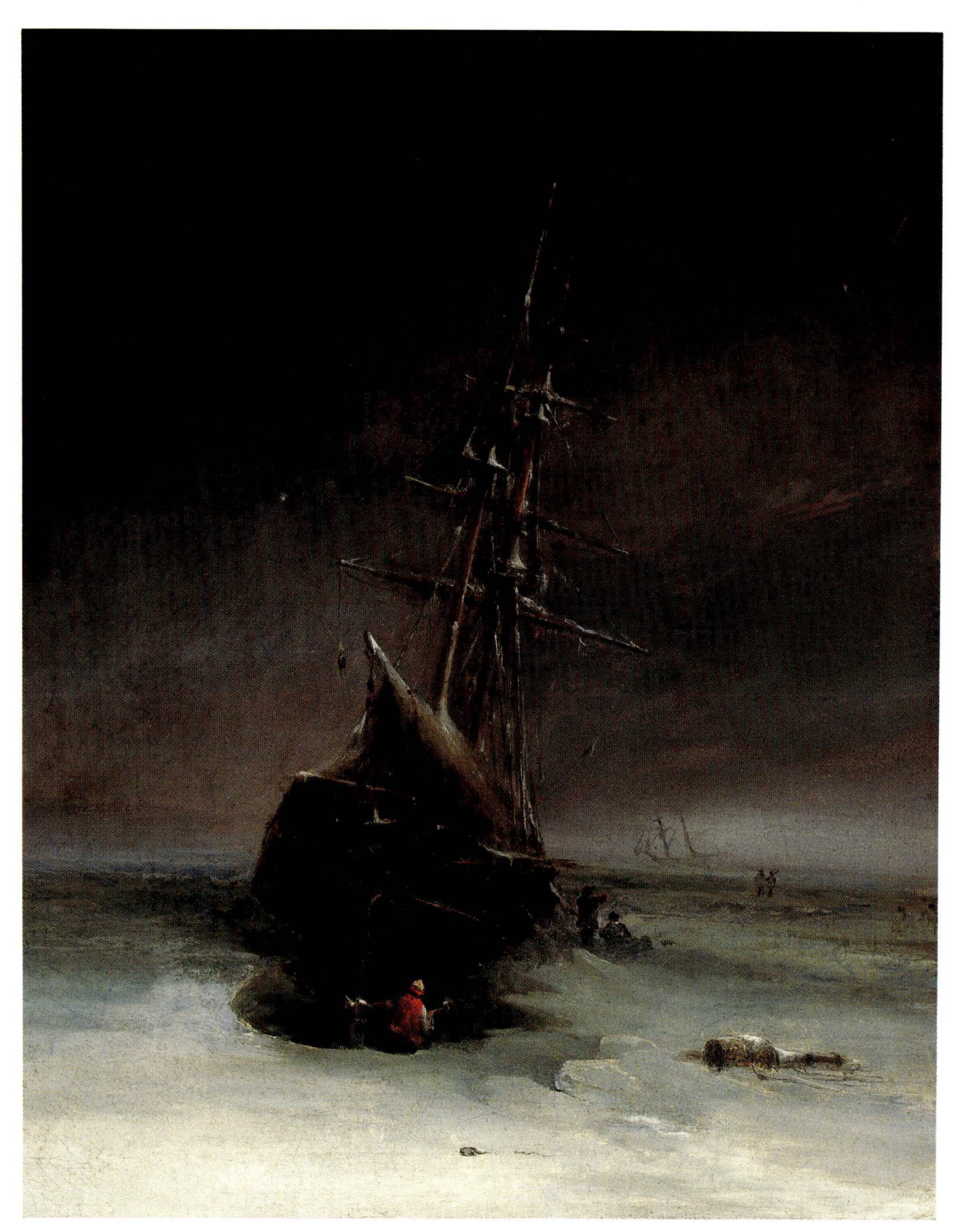

28. James Hamilton
The 'Rescue' in Her Arctic Ice Dock, c. 1852
oil on canvas
91.2 x 74.2 cm
Collection of Seneca Falls Historical Society,
Seneca Falls, New York

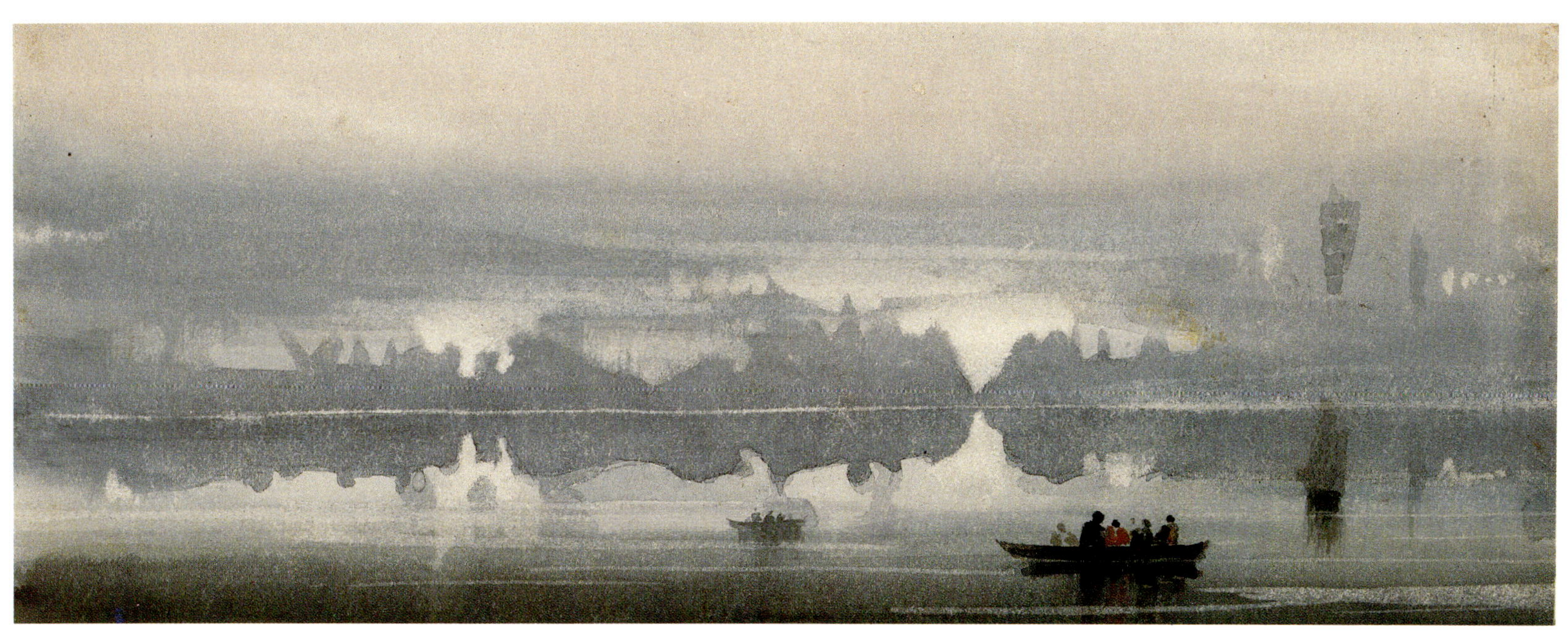

11. James Hamilton
Refraction, c. 1852
watercolour
9.9 x 25.8 cm
Collection of Glenbow Museum

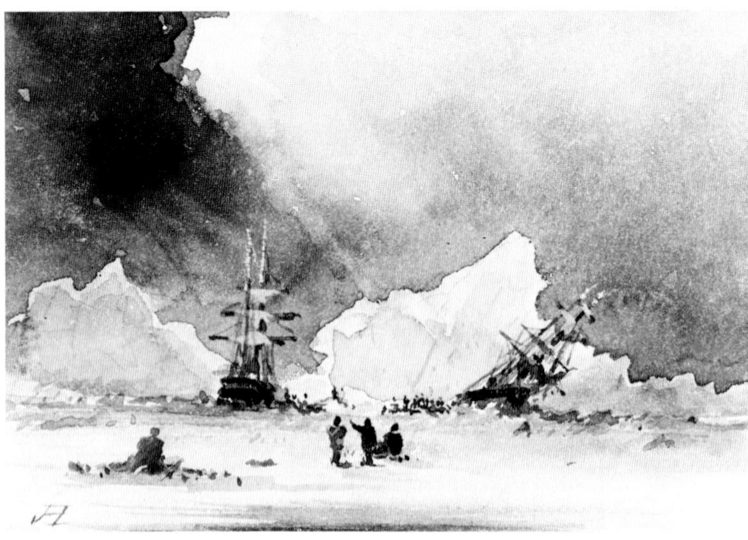

15. James Hamilton
Rescue Nipped, c. 1852
watercolour over pencil
7.7 x 10.8 cm
Collection of Glenbow Museum

Essential to the beauty of the imagery in Kane's books was the quality of the printed illustrations. Both publications employed steel, rather than copper engravings for the principal images. This new process of engraving greatly improved the quality of reproductions.[34] The engraving for Kane's first book was entrusted to Hamilton's mentor, John Sartain. In a letter to Hamilton, Sartain indicated his enthusiasm for the project and agreed to a lower than usual fee for the work. Hamilton in turn, forwarded this letter to Kane with a short note underlining the accord among author, artist and engraver:

John Hamilton Esq:

Dear Sir:

I have considered the proposition of Dr. Kane respecting the Arctic scenes which you submitted to me — namely, to engrave, for the sum of Thirteen Hundred Dollars — ten large subjects — say, eight by twelve inches, and ten small vignettes, similar to the one I am now doing.

I have concluded to reply that I will accept it — my charge or-

dinarily for a similar amount of labour would be nineteen hundred or two thousand dollars, it is therefore clear that the inducement is the opportunity it affords of providing a work that will repay in reputation, and in the pleasure derived from the style and character of the drawings. Whatever costs may be incurred for inscriptions beneath, I of course do not understand as falling upon me.

If the plates are not very well printed the work will reflect no credit on any one, no matter how well engraved. It is therefore necessary that the plates be printed under your eye and mine, and as plate printing can be done in Philadelphia at as little cost as in any other city, there can be no objection I presume. Unless you or I overlook the printing the effect and intention of many of the subjects may be entirely destroyed. I have seen it happen repeatedly.

Yours truly,
John Sartain[35]

Dr. Kane

Dear Sir:

I have pleasure in being able to submit to you the accompanying letter from Mr. Sartain to myself in reply to the offer contained in your note of the 5th instance —

In regard to printing etc. I fully coincide with Mr. Sartain, and I trust that [no] obstacle will exist to prevent Mr. S. and myself exercising exclusive control over not only the printing but also over everything connected with the execution of the undertaking.

Mr. Sartain's feelings and views in relation to the work as expressed to me in conversation, are very similar to my own, with which you are already perfectly familiar.

As I desire to obtain a few proofs of the plates as they progress, please make an arrangement with your publishers to that effect.

Respectfully,
Yours truly,
James Hamilton[36]

Not all of Sartain's and Hamilton's wishes were fulfilled, however, for instead of ten engraved illustrations, *The U.S. Grinnell Expedition* contains only four by Sartain, one directly from Kane's pen, *Striated by Changes of Equilibrium,* and three based on Hamilton's watercolours. The woodblocks, mostly vignettes, number one hundred and twenty-five. None are signed by Hamilton, but five bear the name of Lossing-Barritt, established wood engravers in New York. Added to the edition are eight steam lithographs printed by Duvall and Co. Inferior to the steel and wood engravings in every way, the lithographs are blurred, and possess no depth.

During the preparation of his first book, Kane was unfortunately distracted by other duties. He had been lecturing in an effort to raise support for a second expedition. In one scholarly paper delivered to the American Geographical Society, the explorer expressed his continuing faith in the existence of an Open Polar Sea on whose shores he believed he would discover the lost Franklin party.[37] Before he sailed north from New York on May 31, 1853, aboard the 'Advance', Kane left final arrangements for the completion and publication of his first book with his father, Judge Kane, who as it turned out was to write the last two chapters.[38]

Harper and Brothers, the New York publishers of the 1853 work proved unsatisfactory. In addition to the problem of inferior engravings, disaster struck when the warehouse in which the first printing was stored burned to the ground. Fortunately, a few copies had been forwarded to Judge Kane and printer's plates were safe elsewhere. A second edition appeared a year later in 1854.[39] A comparison between the surviving copies of the 1853 edition and the subsequent reprinting reveal that no changes were made; even the same inferior steam lithographs appear in both.[40] Furthermore, Harper's reduced Kane's fee in order to help pay for the loss of the first printing.

If Kane was disappointed in his relationship with Harper's, he was rewarded by the beautiful, specially bound leather edition with the Kane coat-of-arms which Hamilton presented to him upon his return. Inserted into the book were nineteen original watercolours. Some, identical to the Sartain engravings, provide an accurate means of comparing the artist's and engraver's styles. They also emphasize the technical brilliance of the steel engravings. Some of these presentation watercolours are not included in the printed edition. For example, the work *Crimson Cliffs of Beverley*, records the strange reddish colour of Arctic lichen, a phenomenon called "red snow" which Kane had remarked upon in his journal when visiting the area.[41]

The second book, *Arctic Explorations*, (1856) in two volumes, was placed in the hands of a newly established Philadelphia publisher, Childs and Peterson, and was more elaborate in every way. The publishing firm, hoping to establish its reputation with a best-seller, enhanced the book with twenty-one full-page engrav-

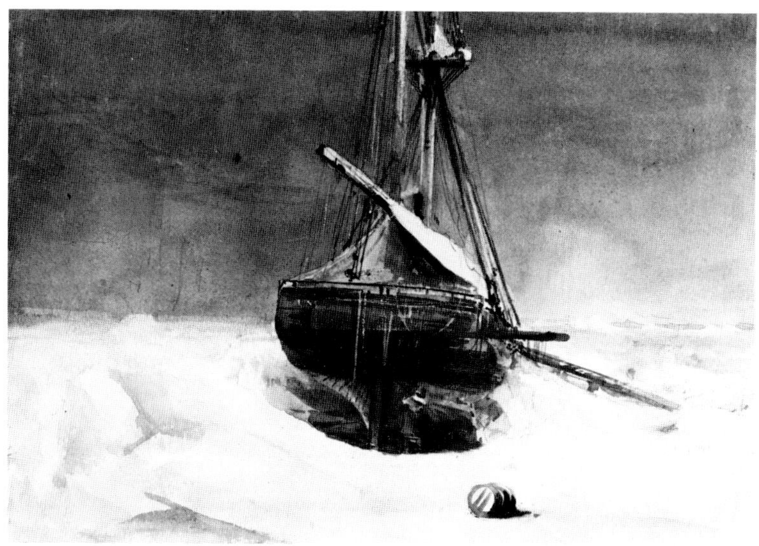

26. James Hamilton
'Rescue' In Her Arctic Ice Dock, 1851, c. 1852
watercolour
23.2 x 31.8 cm
Collection of Mr. Gary Trinetti, Kane, Pa.

ings and 256 vignette woodcuts. John Sartain was not involved in their production. With the help of two additional artists, Mr. White and Christian Schuessele, Hamilton is given credit in the preface as having supervised the whole work. "Although largely, and in some cases exclusively indebted for their interest to the artistic skill of Mr. Hamilton," all work was done primarily from sketches made by Kane on the spot.[42]

Of the twenty-one engravings, including two portraits from daguerreotypes, nineteen are Arctic scenes, seventeen done directly from Kane's sketches. Fifteen of these were based on Hamilton's works and one was done in collaboration with Christian Schuessele. The remaining two are from the hand of Mr. White. These latter appear to have been based on written instructions, for a fragment of a list to Mr. White in Kane's hand instructs the artist to render a particular scene from a description rather than from one of Kane's own drawings.[43] This was also true of Hamilton's depiction of the discovery of the so-called Open Polar Sea at Cape Jefferson. Kane, not being present, had made no sketch.[44] Though the woodcuts in the first publication are not signed, twenty-one in the 1856 volume bear Hamilton's distinctive monogram. *H*

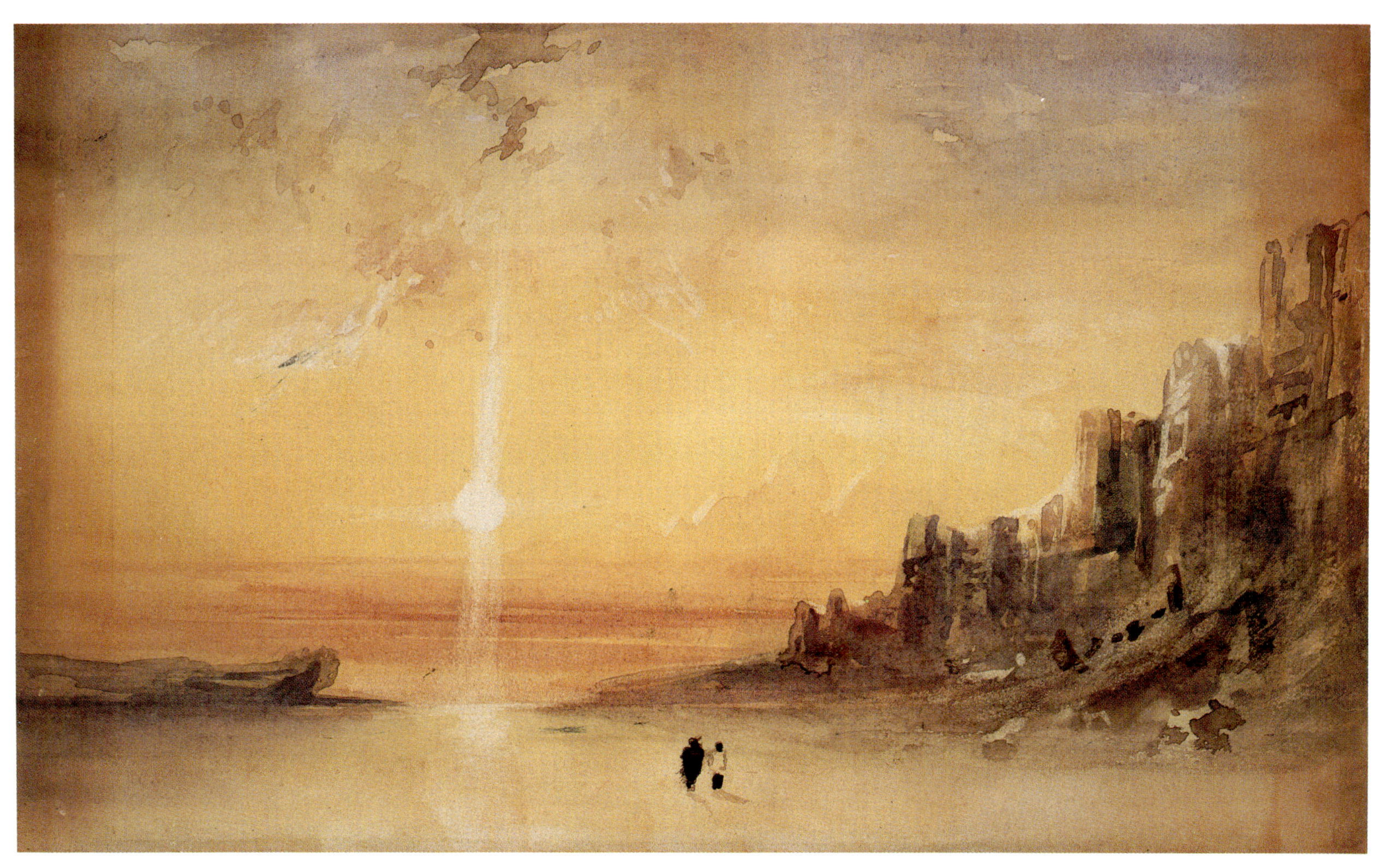

22. James Hamilton
Erebus Bay, Yellow Sunset, c. 1850
watercolour
17.0 x 28.4 cm
Collection of Mrs. W. Beyer Africa, Warren, Pa.

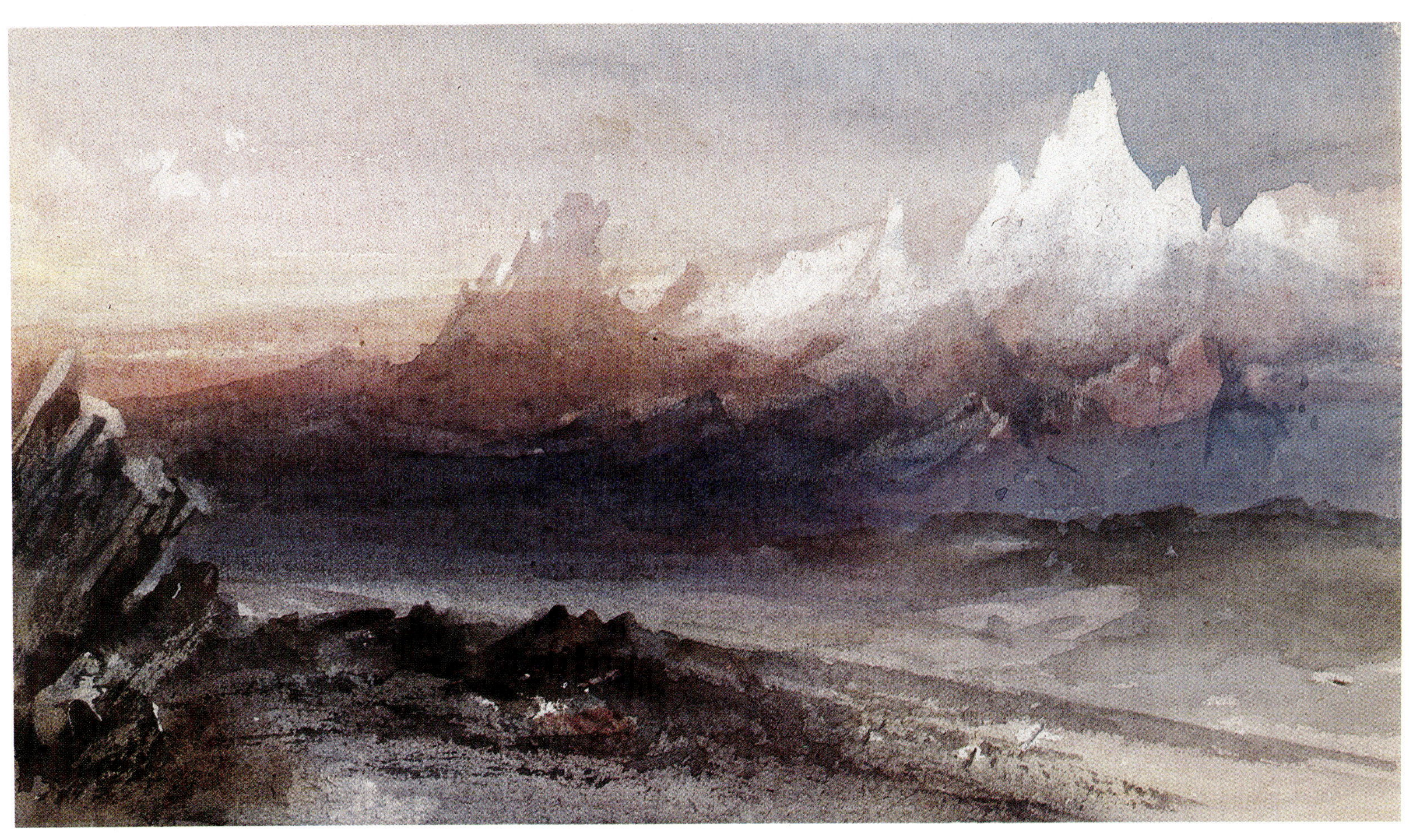

16. James Hamilton
Crimson Cliffs of Beverly, c. 1853
watercolour
12.3 x 21.7 cm
Collection of Library Company, Philadelphia, Pa.

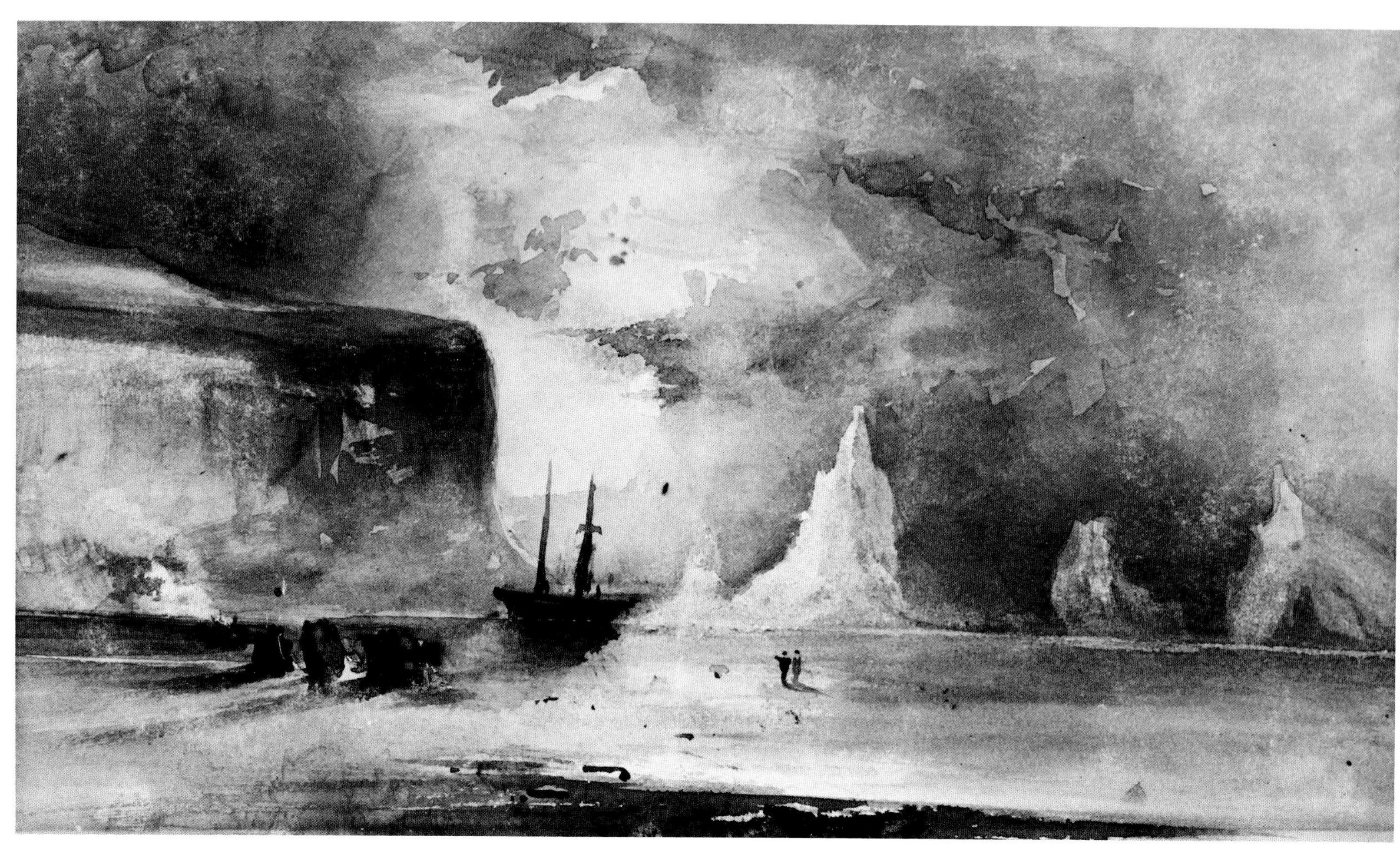

21. James Hamilton
   Beechey Island Graves, 1850, c. 1852
   watercolour
   16.6 x 27.9 cm
   Collection of Mrs. Florence Johnson, Mt. Jewitt, Pa.

The second two volume Arctic narrative was extremely successful, selling 65,000 copies in the first year and netting Kane $65,000.[45] He did not live to realize the gain. Instead, the book was to become his eulogy and the inspiration of future explorers and artists, such as Frederick Edwin Church and William Bradford, who mounted their own expeditions to the Arctic in order to record the northern pole's magnifience.[46]

Although Hamilton enjoyed popular and critical acclaim as an artist during his lifetime, he has long been side-stepped in contemporary art history. It has been difficult to place Hamilton's work in any category. Unlike more familiar names in American art history, such as Thomas Cole, Frederick Edwin Church or William Bradford who produced their paintings from drawings, Hamilton's base, like Turner's, was watercolours. His watercolour style of broad loose strokes survives even when transferred to the precision of steel engravings and woodcut vignettes and was particularly suited to the romantic, picturesque tone of Kane's text.

Popular on both sides of the Atlantic, the Kane-Hamilton colaboration for *Arctic Explorations* received high praise from Blackwell's *Edinburgh Review*. Its comments contain a fitting concluding tribute to Hamilton's artistry:

> the engravings...are eminently happy, as the productions of a man who is a real poet in art, Mr. Hamilton, whose good taste scatters beautiful vignettes, like gems, through the two volumes, and invests the whole work

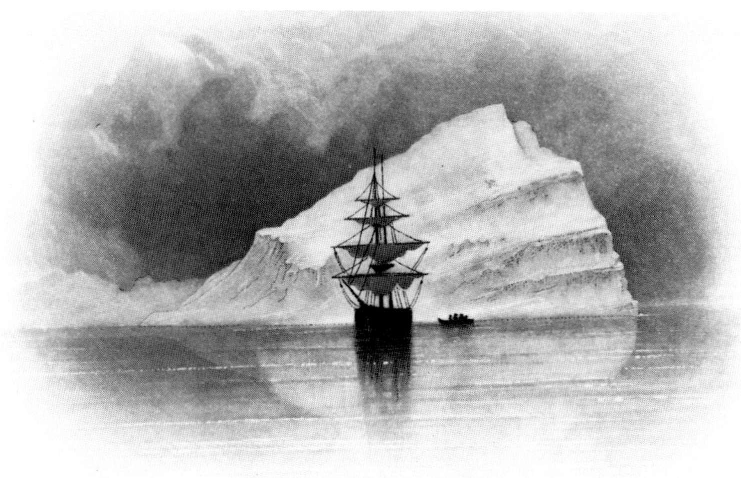

John Sartain
Striated by Changes of Equilibrium, c. 1853
engraving from an original sketch by Dr. Kane from Elisha Kent Kane's;
The U.S. Grinnell Expedition in Search of Sir John Franklin, facing p. 112.

> with a halo of romance, mysterious as the effects of light in those northern regions and which would scarcely have been produced by the power of words, or letter-press unassisted.[47]

Though the Arctic in the next decade continued to be of absorbing interest to American explorers and artists, Hamilton's interests changed. His subjects rooted in nature, remained literary or historical and were reflected in his treatment of such themes as Coleridge's *Ancient Mariner*, an American sea battle, *Action Between the Monitar and Merrimac,* or the romance of the classical world, *The Last Days of Pompeii*, all subjects in keeping with conventional tastes. What set Hamilton apart, however, was his aesthetic contribution: a loose painterly style so unique as to be ahead of its time. This fragile quality especially apparent in his Arctic watercolours, was to disappear from his later work.

Hamilton achieved fame in his own lifetime, but his elusive and inconsistent vision has kept him from a secure place in art history. Yet, it is through the aesthetic properties of his Arctic watercolours commensurate with the explorer's scientific yet romantic quest, that a significant and added dimension to Hamilton's talent is revealed.

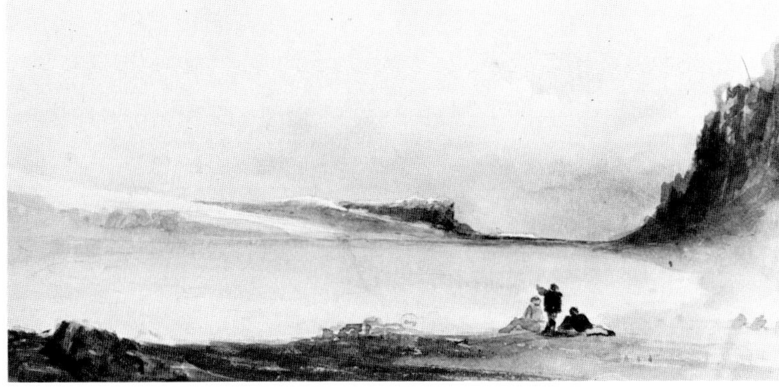

20. James Hamilton
Cape Riley, Erebus Bay, August 27, 1850, c. 1852
watercolour over pencil
10.1 x 20.0 cm
Collection of Glenbow Museum

Notes

1. Mary W. Shelley, *Frankenstein,* (London, 1819), rev. ed. New York: Everyman's Library, *1973, p.3.*

2. Constance Martin, *Perceptions of Arctic Landscapes in the Art of British Explorers, 1818-1859,* (unpublished thesis, 1981), University of Calgary, Chapter 1.

3. Elisha Kent Kane, *The U.S. Grinnell Expedition in Search of Sir John Franklin, 1850-51,* (New York, 1854), p.171.

    Lieutenant William Browne's lithographs were of special interest to Kane as they had met before in the Far East and their paths were to cross again in the Arctic on Beechey Island. "...I was rejoiced to meet an old acquaintance, Lieutenant Browne, whose admirable artistic sketches I had seen in Haghe's lithotints, at Mr. Grinnells, before leaving New York. When we were together last, it was among the tropical jungles of Luzon..."

4. Chauncey C. Loomis, *Wierd and Tragic Shores: The Story of Charles Francis Hall, Explorer,* (New York, 1971), pp.39-40.

5. Martin, p.55.

6. This latter was the spot from which Robert Peary was to make his final sprint to the North Pole in 1909.

7. Charles Francis Hall, *Life with the Esquimaux,* (New York, 1865).

8. George W. Corner, *Doctor Kane of the Arctic Seas,* (Philadelphia, 1972), p.167.

9. Ibid., p.167, "Polynia" or "Polynya," a Russian term for an open water space.

10. Ibid., p.168.

11. William Elder, *Biography of Elisha Kent Kane,* (Philadelphia, 1858), p.216.

12. Ibid., p.216.

13. Ibid., pp.216-218.

14. John Sartain, "James Hamilton," *Sartain's Union Magazine of Literature and Art,* vol. 10 (1852) p.332.

15. Anna Wells Rutledge, *Cumulative Record of Exhibition Catalogues, The Pennsylvania Academy of the Fine Arts 1807-1870,* (Philadelphia, 1955), p.88.

16. Quoted in Arlene Jacobowitz's *James Hamilton, (1819-1878)* Exhibition catalogue, Brooklyn Museum, 1966, p.22 *(Progressive fragments Drawn and Etched in a Broad and Simple Manner, Easy Lessons in Landscape Drawing, Hints on Light, and Shadow, Composition, etc. as Applicable to Landscape Painting, and Sketches at Home and Abroad — Hints on the Acquirement of Freedom of Execution and Breadth of Effect in Landscape Painting.)*

17. Sartain, p.332.

18. E.(mily) S.(artain), *Catalogue of Painting: From the Studio of James Hamilton, P.A., Under the Direction of Messrs. James S. Earle & Sons,* (Philadelphia, 1875), p.2.

19. Theodore E. Stebbins, Jr., *American Master Drawings and Watercolours,* (New York, 1975), p.148.

20. Jacobowitz, p.13.

21. Sartain, p.331.

22. E(mily) S(artain), p.2.

23. Ibid., p.1.

24. New York *Herald Tribune,* "James Hamilton", August 21, 1866, p.2.

25. Sartain, p.332.

26. Kane, *U.S. Grinnell Expedition,* (1854), pp.63-69.

27. Elder, p.219.

28. Quoted in Elder, Ibid., p.221.

29. Kane, *U.S. Grinnell Expedition,* (1854), p.59.

30. Ibid., pp.75-77.

31. Elisha Kent Kane, *Arctic Explorations: The Second Grinnell Expedition in Search of Sir John Franklin, 1853, '54, '55,* Vol. II, (Philadelphia, 1856), p.57.

32. Kane, *U.S. Grinnell Expedition,* (1854), pp.63-69.

33. Ibid., p.162.

34. F. Weitenkampt, *American Graphic Art,* (New York, 1924), p.77. The steel engraving process had been developed in the United States to meet the demand for high quality bank notes to make counterfeiting more difficult. Ever practical and resourceful, American printers had turned the process to good use in book engravings.

35. John Sartain, Letter to James Hamilton, October 9, 1852, American Philosophical Society Library, Philadelphia.

36. James Hamilton, Letter to Elisha Kent Kane, October 11, 1852, American Philosophical Society Library, Philadelphia.

37. Elisha Kent Kane, "Access to An Open Polar Sea," American Geographical and Statistical Society, (New York, 1853).

38. Corner, pp.263-264.

39. Edwin Wolf, and Elena Korey editors, *Quarter of a Millenium 1731-1981,* Library Co., (Philadelphia, 1981), p.319.

40. Elisha Kent Kane, *The U.S. Grinnell Expedition in Search of Sir John Franklin, 1850-51,* (New York, 1854).

41. Ibid., see catalogue number 16.

42. Kane, *Arctic Explorations,* Vol. I, pp.5-6.

43. Elisha Kent Kane, instructions to Mr. White, New York Public Library Manuscript, Miscellaneous

    "Mr. White will oblige me by making up at his earliest convenience
    1. A powerful team of seven Esquimaux dogs — very wolfish in character..."

44. Kane, *Arctic Explorations,* facing page 307, under the title of the engraving, "From description".

45. Elder, pp.224-225.

46. Frederick Edwin Church sailed to Labrador and Newfoundland in 1859. He was the first of the American painters to journey north on his own. William Bradford made a series of voyages for the same artistic purposes, beginning in 1861. One of these voyages in 1869 included Dr. Isaac Hayes, the surgeon of Kane's 1853-55 expedition. Hayes own expedition in 1860, supported by Henry Grinnell and Church had continued Kane's search for an open polar sea. Included in his publication of the journey, *Open Polar Sea,* is an illustration of the mountain Hayes named for Church, *Church's Peak.* This in turn became Church's inspiration for one of his famous Arctic paintings, *Aurora Borealis.*

47. *Blackwood's Edinburgh Magazine,* November 1855, p.373.

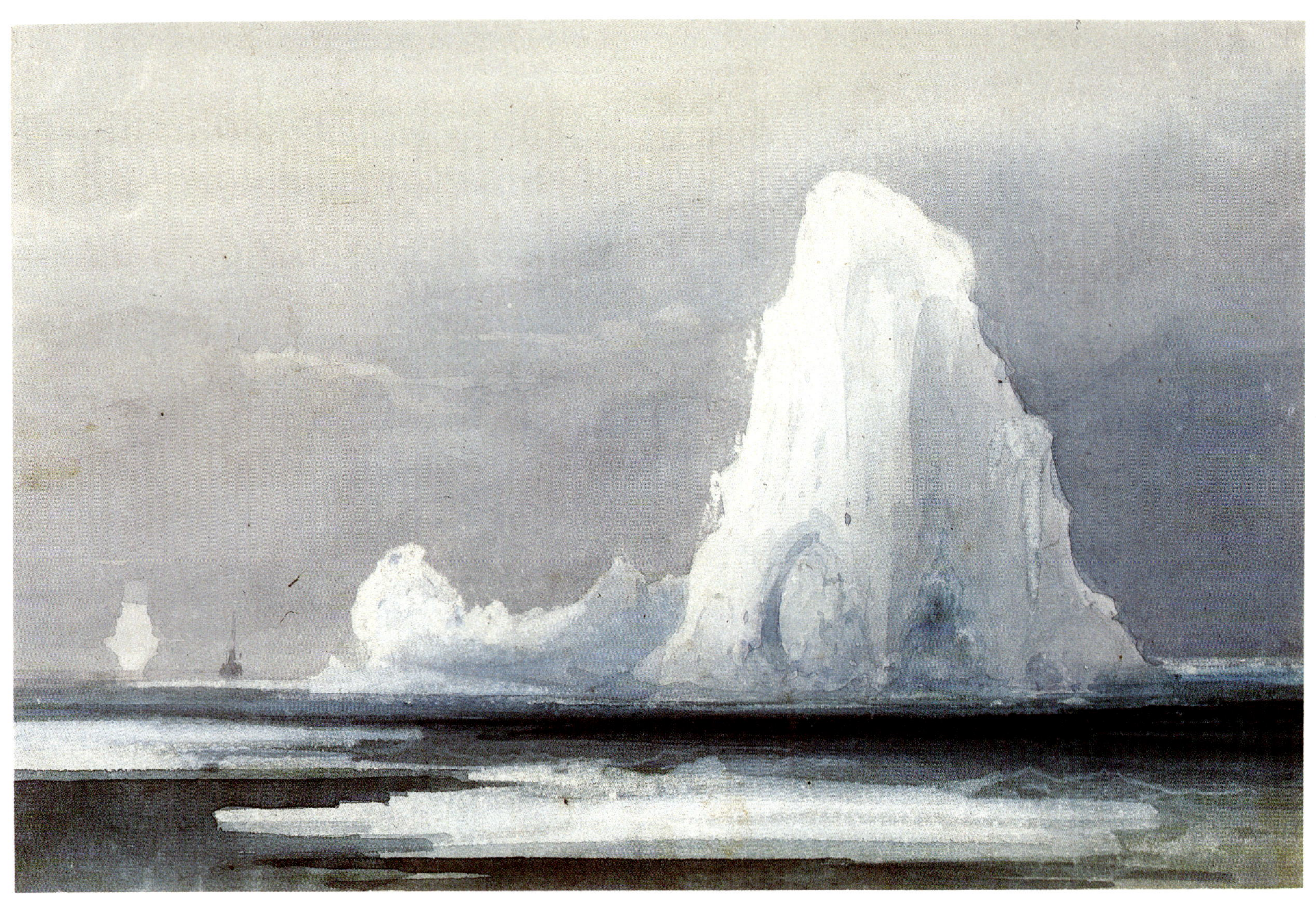

10. James Hamilton
Berg off Cape Melville, n.d.
watercolour
17.5 x 26.6 cm
Collection of Glenbow Museum

Selected Bibliography

Baur, John I.H. "A Romantic Impressionist: James Hamilton." *The Brooklyn Museum Bulletin,* Vol. XII, no. 3, Spring 1951, pp. 1-8.

Blackwood's Edinburg Magazine, "Arctic Adventure." March 1857, pp. 366-379.

Browne, W.H. *Ten Coloured Views Taken During the Arctic Expeditions of Her Majesty's Ships 'Enterprise' and 'Investigator'...with a Summary of the Various Arctic Expeditions in Search of Capt. Sir John Franklin.* London: Ackermann & Co., 1850.

Corner, George. *Doctor Kane of the Arctic Seas.* Philadelphia: Temple University Press, 1972.

Elder, William. *Biography of Elisha Kent Kane.* Philadelphia: Childs and Peterson, 1858.

Frost, John. *The Pictorial History of the American Navy: Comprising Lives of its Distinguished Commanders...,* (New York, 1854), p. 6.

Hall, Charles Francis. *Life with the Esquimaux.* New York: Harper and Bros., 1865; reprint, Charles E. Tuttle Co., 1970.

Hamilton, Sinclair. *Early American Book Illustrators and Wood Engravers 1670-1870.* Princeton, 1958.

Hayes, Issac I. M.D. *The Open Polar Sea, A Narrative of a Voyage of Discovery Towards the North Pole.* New York: Hurd and Houghton, 1867.

Jacobowitz, Arlene. *James Hamilton, 1819-1878.* The Brooklyn Museum Special Exhibition Catalogue, (March 28-May 22, 1966).

Kane, Elisha Kent. *U.S. Grinnell Expedition in Search of Sir John Franklin, 1850-51.* New York: Harper Bros., 1853.

Kane, Elisha Kent. *U.S. Grinnell Expedition in Search of Sir John Franklin, 1850-51.* New York: Harper Bros., 1854.

Kane, Elisha Kent. *Arctic Explorations: Second Grinnell Expedition in Search of Sir John Franklin, 1853, '54. '55.* Philadelphia: Childs & Peterson, 1856.

Kane, Elisha Kent. "Access to an Open Polar Sea." *American Geographical and Statistical Society,* New York: Baker, Godwin & Co., 1853.

Kane, Elisha Kent. Manuscript Collection, Miscellaneous. New York: New York City Public Library.

Knoepflmacher, U.C. & Tennyson G.B. (ed.). *Nature and the Victorian Imagination.* Chauncey C. Loomis, "The Arctic Sublime," p. 100, Berkeley, California: University of California Press, 1977.

Loomis, Chauncey C. *Weird and Tragic Shores: The Story of Charles Francis Hall, Explorer.* New York: Alfred A. Knopf, 1971.

New York Herald Tribune, "James Hamilton," August 21, 1866, p. 2.

Novak, Barbara. *Nature and Culture: American Landscape and Painting 1825-1875.* New York: Oxford University Press, 1980.

Rutledge, Anna Wells. *Cumulative Record of Exhibition Catalogues, The Pennsylvania Academy of the Fine Arts 1807-1870.* Philadelphia: The American Philosophical Society, 1955.

Shelley, Mary. *Frankenstein.* London: 1819, ed. New York: Everyman's Library, 1973.

Shephard, L.A. *American Painters of the Arctic.* Exhibition Catalogue, Mead Art Gallery, Amherst College; Amherst, Massachusetts, 1975.

Stebbins, Jr. *Theodore E., American Master Drawings and Watercolours.* New York: Harper & Row, 1976.

S.(artain), E.(mily). *Catalogue of Paintings: From the Studio of James Hamilton, P.A. Under the Direction of Messrs. James S. Earle & Sons.* (Philadelphia, 1875).

Sartain, John. "James Hamilton." *Sartain's Union Magazine of Literature and Art,* vol. 10, 1852, p. 332.

Weitenkampt, F. *American Graphic Art.* New York: 1924.

Wilmerding, John. *William Bradford.* Exhibition Catalogue, Decordova Museum, (Lincoln, Mass., 1970), Whaling Museum, New Bedford, Mass., 1970.

Wilmerding, John. *American Light: The Luminist Movement, 1850-1875.* Exhibition Catalogue, National Gallery of Art, Washington, D.C. 1980.

Wolf, Edwin, Marie Elena Korey editors. *Quarter of a Millenium.* Philadelphia: Library Company, 1981.

Appendix

Illustrated Arctic
Narratives
1773-1862

Phillips, Constantine, J. *A Voyage Towards the North Pole, 1773.* London: J. Nourse, 1774.

Ross, John. *Voyage of Discovery.* London: Longmans, 1819.

Parry, William Edward. *...For Discovery of Northwest Passage from Atlantic to Pacific 1819-20 ... on 'Hecla' & 'Griper'.* London: John Murray, 1821.

Franklin, John. *Narrative of a Journey to the Shores of the Polar Sea in the Years 1819, '20, '21, and '22.* London: John Murray, 1823. Reprint, Edmonton: M.G. Hurtig, 1969.

Lyon, G.F. *Private Journal of Capt. G.F. Lyon, H.M.S. 'Hecla'.* London: John Murray, 1824.

Parry, William Edward. *Second Voyage for Discovery of the Northwest Passage from the Atlantic to the Pacific, 1821, '22, '23.* London: J. Murray, 1824.

Franklin, John. *Narrative of a Second Expedition to the Shores of the Polar Sea in the Years 1825, 1826, and 1827.* London: John Murray, 1828.

Beechey, F.W. *Voyage of Discovery . . . North Pole . . . H.M.S. 'Dorothea' and 'Trent'.* London: Bentley, 1843.

Ross, John. *Narrative of a Second Voyage in Search of a Northwest Passage 1829-1833.* London: A.W. Webster, 1835.

Back, George. *Journal to the Great Fish River, 1833, '34, '35, Along the Shores of the Arctic Ocean.* London: John Murray, 1836.

Back, George. *Narrative of the Expedition in the H.M.S. 'Terror'* London: John Murray, 1838.

Browne, W.H. *Ten Coloured Views Taken During the Arctic Expeditions of Her Majesty's Ships 'Enterprise' and 'Investigator' . . . with a Summary of the . . . Search of Capt. Sir John Franklin.* London: Ackermann & Co., 1850.

Snow, William Parker. *Voyage of the Prince Albert in Search of Sir John Franklin: A Narrative of Every-Day Life in the Arctic Seas.* London: Longman, Brown & Green, 1851.

Osborn, Sherard. *Discovery of the Northwest Passage by . . . 'Investigator' 1850, '51, '52, '53, '54.* London: Longmans, 3rd ed., 1859.

Osborn, Sherard and McDougall, F.M. *Facsimile of the Illustrated Arctic News.* London: Ackermann & Co., 1852.

McDougall, George F. *H.M.S. Discovery Ship 'Resolute' to Arctic . . . Search for Franklin and the Missing Crews of . . . 'Erebus' & 'Terror', 1852, '53, '54.* London: Longmans, Brown, 1857.

McCormick, R. *Narrative of a Boat Expedition up Wellington Channel.* London: George Edward Eyre & William Spottiswood, 1854.

Kane, Elisha Kent. *U.S. Grinnell Expedition in Search of Sir John Franklin.* New York: Harper Bros., 1854.

Cresswell, S.G. *Series of Eight Sketches in Colour Lithographs for the Queen, Voyage of 'Investigator'.* no. pub., 1854.

May, W.W. *Series of Fourteen Sketches Made During the Voyage Up Wellington Channel in Search of Sir John Franklin . . . Together with a Short Account of Each Drawing.* London: 1855.

Kane, Elisha Kent. *Arctic Explorations: Second Grinnell Expedition in Search of . . . Franklin, 1853, '54, '55.* Philadelphia: Childs & Peterson, 1856.

McClintock, Francis Leopold. *The Voyage of the 'Fox' in the Arctic Seas: A Narrative of the Discovery of the Fate of Sir John Franklin and His Companions.* Boston: Ticknor & Fields, 1860.

Hayes, Isaac I., M.D. *An Open Polar Sea, A Narrative of a Voyage of Discovery Towards the North Pole.* New York: Hurd and Houghton, 1867.

Hall, Charles Francis. *Life with the Esquimaux.* New York: Harper and Bros., 1865; reprint, Charles E. Tuttle Co., 1970.

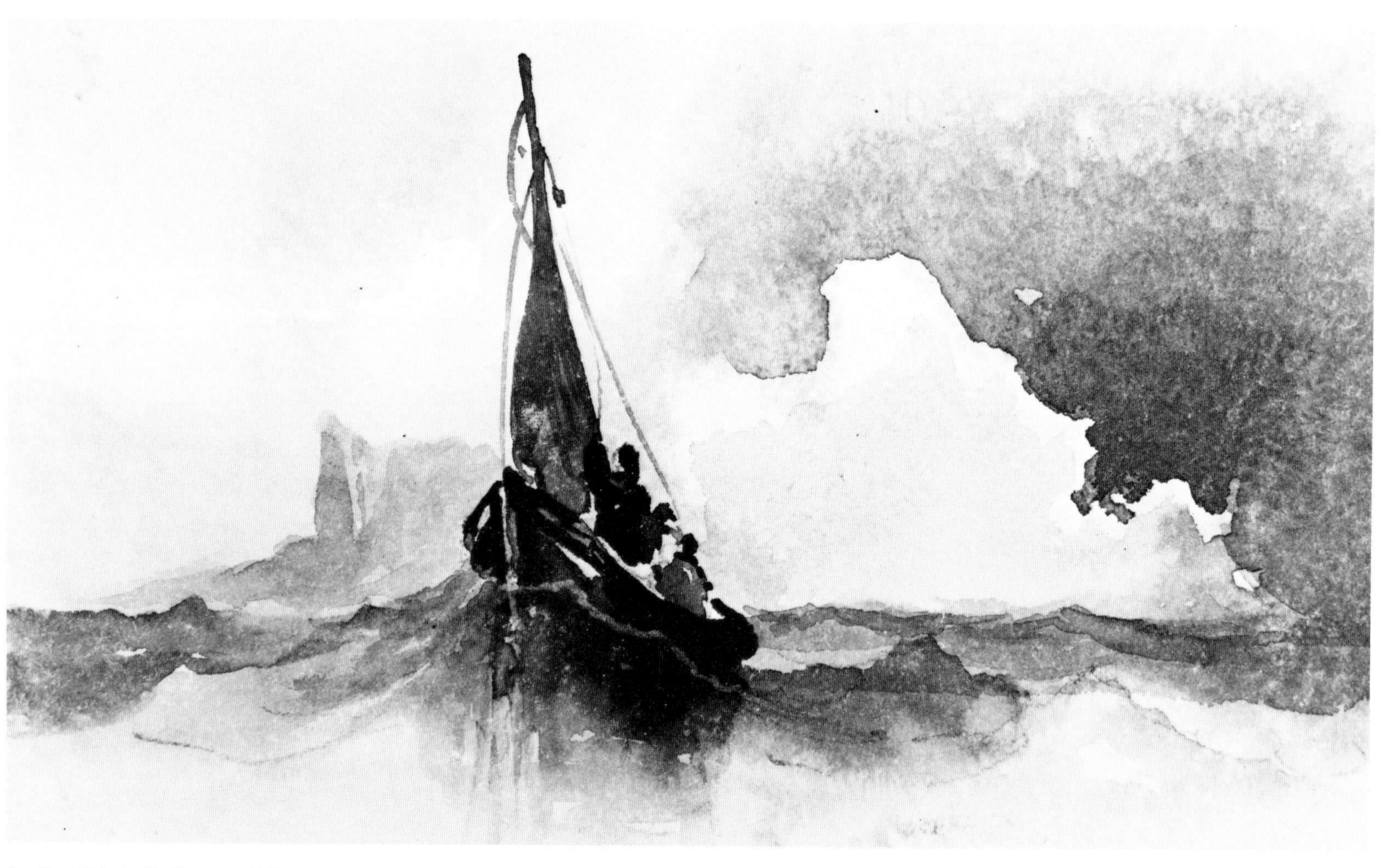

5. *Boat Trip to Godhaven*, c.1850

Catalogue of the Exhibition

The following works are listed in chronological order as nearly as possible according to events as they occured in the expeditions.

Those in the Glenbow Collection as well as those on loan are predominantly related to Elisha Kent Kane's book, *U.S. Grinnell Expedition in Search of Sir John Franklin.*, (1854); only a few are associated with Kane's other narrative *Arctic Explorations, 1853, '54, '55,* (1856), the explorer's second and last expedition.

All dimensions are given in centimetres, height precedes width. Works in the collection of Glenbow Museum include catalogue numbers. Works illustrated are marked with an asterisk.*

1. William Browne
   (d. 1872)
   Termination of Cliffs Near Whaler Point, Port Leopold
   c. 1849
   lithograph
   20.0 x 60.3 image
   37.5 x 27.5 sheet

   Provenance: Henry Stevens, Surrey, England
   Folio Edition: *Ten Coloured Views Taken During the Arctic Expedition of Her Majesty's Ships 'Enterprise' and 'Investigator',* (London, 1850)

   Collection of Glenbow Museum
   70.7.1.6   *Page 10

2. James Hamilton
   (1819-1878)
   One of the Ships of the Grinnell Expedition
   c.1852
   oil on wood
   29.3 x 44.5 (sight)
   Verso: "One of the ships of the Grinnell Expedition in Search of Sir John Franklin By James Hamilton (1819-1878). Presented to Cornelius Grinnell by Dr. Elisha Kent Kane, the leader of the expedition."

   Provenance: Grinnell Family
   Kennedy Galleries, Inc., New York
   Exhibition: *James Hamilton*, Brooklyn Museum, 1966
   American Painters of the Arctic,
   Amherst College, Amherst, Massachusetts, 1975
   Bibliography: The Kennedy Quarterly (bibl. 29, 1964), p.272, no.595

   The title and inscription were probably added later for the following reasons: The image, though titled *One of the Ships of the Grinnell Expedition* depicts two ships. This would relate the scene to the first voyage of 1850-51, which was led by Lieut. de Haven with Elisha Kent Kane as surgeon. Kane led the second Grinnell expedition of 1853-55 and sailed with one ship only — the 'Advance'. The date is therefore more likely to be c.1852 rather than c.1857 as previously recorded in the Brooklyn Museum catalogue.
   Appears related to Chapter III, *U.S. Grinnell Expedition,* (1854), June 7, 1850: "With the 7th of June came fine, bright, bracing weather. We were off Newfoundland, getting along

well over a smooth sea ...when about noon, a great mass of whiteness was seen floating in the sunshine. It was our first iceberg. It was in shape an oblong cube, and about twice as large as Girard College. Its colour was an unmixed, but not dazzling white: indeed, it seemed entirely coated with snow of such unsullied, unreflecting purity, that, as we passed within a hundred yards of it, not a glitter reached us. It reminded me of a great marble monolith, only awaiting the chisel to stand out in peristyle and pediment a floating Parthenon. There was something very imposing in the impassive tranquillity with which it received the lashings of the sea," p.27.

Collection of Mrs. Robert S. Grinnell, New York.   *Page 13

3. James Hamilton
    (1819-1878)
    Ships and Kayak in Moonlight
    c.1852
    watercolour
    10.1 x 16.1
    Verso: "Composition by Hamilton #14"

    Provenance: Hilda France (N.J.)
                Kennedy Galleries, Inc., New York

    Collection of Glenbow Museum
    60.22.9

4. James Hamilton
    (1819-1878)
    Two Ships
    c.1852
    watercolour
    18.4 x 24.7 sheet
    6.3 x 14.0 image
    Verso: "#10"

    Provenance: Hilda France (N.J.)
                Kennedy Galleries, Inc., New York
    Composition appears several times as an engraving and wood-cut with variations, in both *U.S. Grinnell Expedition*, (1854), pages 23 and 28, and *Arctic Explorations*, (1856), frontispiece.

    Collection of Glenbow Museum
    60.22.10

5. James Hamilton
    (1819-1878)
    Boat Trip to Godhaven
    c.1850
    watercolour over pencil
    6.5 x 12.7
    Verso: "Composition Boat Trip to Godhaven #27"

    Provenance: Hilda France (N.J.)
                Kennedy Galleries, Inc., New York
    Relates to Chapter VI in *U.S. Grinnell Expedition* (1854) in which Kane describes sailing from Crown Prince Islands to neighbouring Lively, (Godhaven) on Disko Island, the Danish settlement, to collect information and purchase furs, June 27, 1850. pp.43-49.

    Collection of Glenbow Museum
    60.22.8

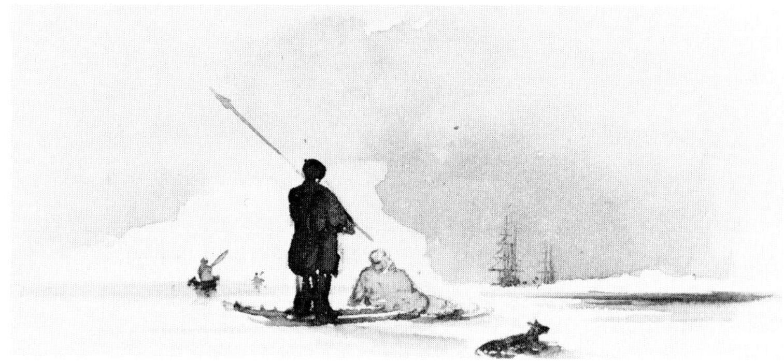

6. *Holsteinberg*, n.d.

6. James Hamilton
    (1819-1878)
    Holsteinberg
    n.d.
    watercolour over pencil
    6.6 x 13.0
    Verso: "Holsteinberg #36"

    Provenance: Hilda France (N.J.)
                Kennedy Galleries, Inc., New York
    One of two Danish inspectorates for the Danish coast of Greenland, the other being Lively. See *North End of Leifley*.

    Collection of Glenbow Museum
    60.22.18

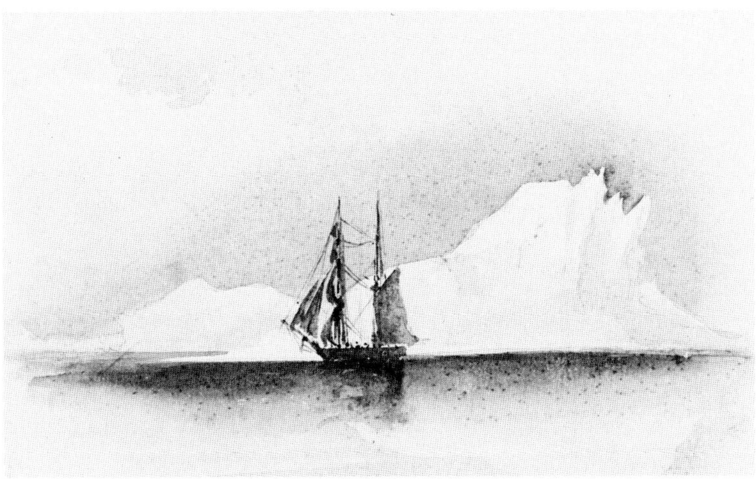

9. *Advance with Iceberg*, c. 1852

7. James Hamilton
    (1819-1878)
    North End of Leifley (Godhaven)
    c. 1852
    watercolour
    8.1 x 12.7
    Signed 1.1.: J.H.
    Verso: "North End of Leifley #8"

    Provenance: Hilda France (N.J.)
    Kennedy Galleries, Inc., New York
    Relates to Chapter VI, *U.S. Grinnell Expedition*, (1854). "This little port of Lievely or Godhaven is on a gneissoid spur, offsetting from the larger mass of Disco...Disco is the largest circumnavigable island on the coast of Greenland..." p. 47. "This was the house of the 'Royal Inspector of the Northern portions of Davis's Straits;' There are but two inspectorates for the Danish coast of Greenland: one termed the Southern, whose centre is Holsteinberg; the other the Northern, whose seat is Lievely." pp. 44-45.

    Collection of Glenbow Museum
    60.22.15

8. Elisha Kent Kane
    (1820-1857)
    Sailboat
    n.d.
    pencil and ink
    15.3 x 11.6

    Collection of American Philosophical Society, Philadelphia, Pa.

9. James Hamilton
    (1819-1878)
    Advance with Iceberg
    c. 1852
    watercolour over pencil
    10.4 x 17.0
    Verso: "July 1850 #9"

    Provenance: Hilda France (N.J.)
    Kennedy Galleries, Inc., New York
    Related to Chapter VIII, *U.S. Grinnell Expedition* (1854), concerning the formation of icebergs. pp. 56-62.

    Collection of Glenbow Museum
    60.22.7

10. James Hamilton
    (1819-1878)
    Berg off Cape Melville
    n.d.
    watercolour
    17.5 x 26.7
    Verso: "Berg off Cape Melville #29"

    Provenance: Hilda France (N.J.)
    Kennedy Galleries, Inc., New York
    Relates to Chapter IX, *U.S. Grinnell Expedition*, (1854). "An iceberg is one of God's own buildings, preaching its lessons of humility to the miniature structures of man. Its material, one colossal Pentelicus; its mass, the representative of power in repose; its distribution, simulating every architectural type." p. 67-68.

    Collection of Glenbow Museum
    60.22.19   *Page 29

11. James Hamilton
(1819-1878)
Refraction
c.1852
watercolour
9.9 x 25.8
Verso: "Refraction #17"

Provenance: Hilda France (N.J.)
            Kennedy Galleries, Inc., New York
Refers to Chapter IX, *U.S. Grinnell Expedition*, (1854). July 4th "Toward 11 P.M. the temperature of the water fell to 30°, while that of the air rose to 36° and 37°. Looking toward the shore, I observed a sort of shimmering, as of the heated air above a stove, and at the same time, the base of the hills assumed a columnar character, as marked as in the basalts of Staffa. Soon afterward, the entire land came up to us through a highly refractive medium, and the vertical arrangement which had displayed itself before in columns was broken into waving curves, the parallelism of their lines remaining unchanged. As the sun reached his greatest meridional depression, this was accompanied by an extreme distortion. The homogeneous character of the atmosphere was singularly disturbed. It was like gazing at a panorama through badly blown and uneven glass ...The little islands about the shore were elevated into Champagne bottles and mushrooms...A thousand forms, inverted, looming, and distorted most extravagantly, were shifting about within an arc of ten degrees of coast." pp. 64-65.

Collection of Glenbow Museum
60.22.12

*Page 21

12. James Hamilton
(1819-1878)
Refraction
n.d.
watercolour
9.0 x 17.2
Verso: "Refraction #15"

Provenance: Hilda France (N.J.)
            Kennedy Galleries, Inc., New York

Collection of Glenbow Museum
60.22.5

13. James Hamilton
(1819-1878)
Melville Bay
n.d.
watercolour
9.0 x 20.5 image
16.9 x 27 sheet
Signed l.r.: "J. Hamilton"
Verso: "Melville Bay #33"

Provenance: Hilda France (N.J.)
            Kennedy Galleries, Inc., New York
Related to Chapter XIII, *U.S. Grinnell Expedition,* (1854). "It is during the transit of this bay that most of the catastrophes occur which have made the statistics of the whalers so fearful. It was here, that in one year more than one thousand human beings were cast shelterless upon the ice, their ships ground up before their eyes. It is rarely that a season goes by in which the passage is attempted without disaster." pp. 102-103.

Collection of Glenbow Museum
60.22.20

*Page 18

14. Elisha Kent Kane
(1820-1857)
Cape Melville, August 14, 1850
pencil and watercolour
17.6 x 27.6
Recto: below image centre: "Cape — N.E. by N. (Time) — Cape Melville" l.l.: "Note — The Ravine X is about 600 feet deep yet no apparent Glacier action at base! Sky clear blue water which [*sic*] Mackerel stratus seen." l.r.: "X Glacier with fractured surface X from which has recently separated the Iceberg — A — still visible — when sketched August 14. 50 10.a.m."
Verso: "Iceberg resembling the fyne [*sic*] portico of the Rameseum", with small sketch.

Relates to Chapter XVII of *U.S. Grinnell Expedition*, (1854) "August 14, . . . We ran along the coast to-day with gentle airs, and near enough to keep me busy with my pencil. Glacier after glacier met us, and the background of rounding snow-covered mountains contrasted finely with the square blocking of the rugged precipices at the water-line." p. 130

Collection of American Philosophical Society, Philadelphia, Pa.

15. James Hamilton
(1819-1878)
Rescue Nipped
c.1852
watercolour over pencil
7.7 x 10.8
Signed l.l.: "J.H." [in monogram]
Verso: "Rescue Nipped 1 #4"

Provenance: Hilda France (N.J.)
           Kennedy Galleries, Inc., New York
Nipped by the ice on August, 1850 the 'Rescue' proved to be less manoeuverable in Arctic waters than the larger leadship 'Advance'.
This watercolour appears to be the inspiration for John Sartain's engraving in *U.S. Grinnell Expedition* (1854), facing page 120 and related to Hamilton's oil painting *Breaking Up of an Iceberg in Melville Bay.*

Collection of Glenbow Museum
60.22.23   *Page 22

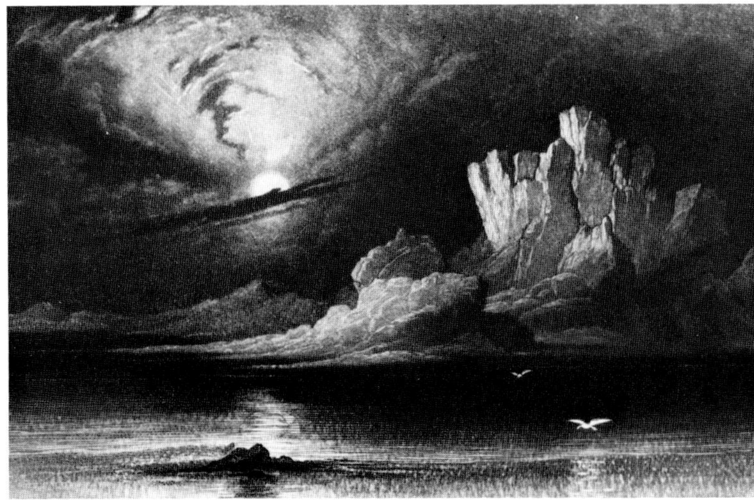

18. *Grounded Berg Near Cape York*, c.1853

16. James Hamilton
(1819-1878)
Crimson Cliffs of Beverly
c.1853
watercolour
12.3 x 21.7

Provenance: Kane Family
           Mr. Robert Gray Taylor
Exhibition: *James Hamilton*, Brooklyn Museum, 1966
One of the 19 paintings of a unique special bound edition of Elisha Kent Kane's *U.S. Grinnell Expedition* (1854); opp. p.135

Relates to Chapter XVIII. Like his sketches, Kane's vivid descriptive prose was an inspiration for Hamilton's watercolours: "In a short time we reached the 'Crimson Cliffs of Beverly', the seat of the often-described 'red snow'...we found the red snow in greatest abundance upon a talus fronting to the southwest, which stretched obliquely across the glacier...Its colour was a deep but not bright red. It resembled, with its accompanying impurities, crushed preserved cranberries with the seed and capsule strewn over the snow. It imparted to paper drawn over it a nearly cherry-red, or perhaps crimson stain, which became brown with exposure; and a handful thawed in a glass tumbler resembled muddy claret. Its colouring matter was evidently soluble; for, on scraping away the surface, we found that it had dyed the snow beneath with a pure and beautiful rose colour, which penetrated, with a gradually softening tint, some eight inches below the surface," pp.139-140.

Collection of Library Company, Philadelphia, Pa.   *Page 25

17. James Hamilton
(1819-1878)
Grounded Berg Near Cape York
c.1853
watercolour
12.3 x 21.7

Provenance: Kane Family
           Mr. Robert Gray Taylor
One of 19 paintings of a unique specially bound edition of Elisha Kent Kane's *U.S. Grinnell Expedition*, (1854); facing p.142.
Kane challenged the illustrator in this description of the scene: "Though I had read a good deal in the voyagers' books about

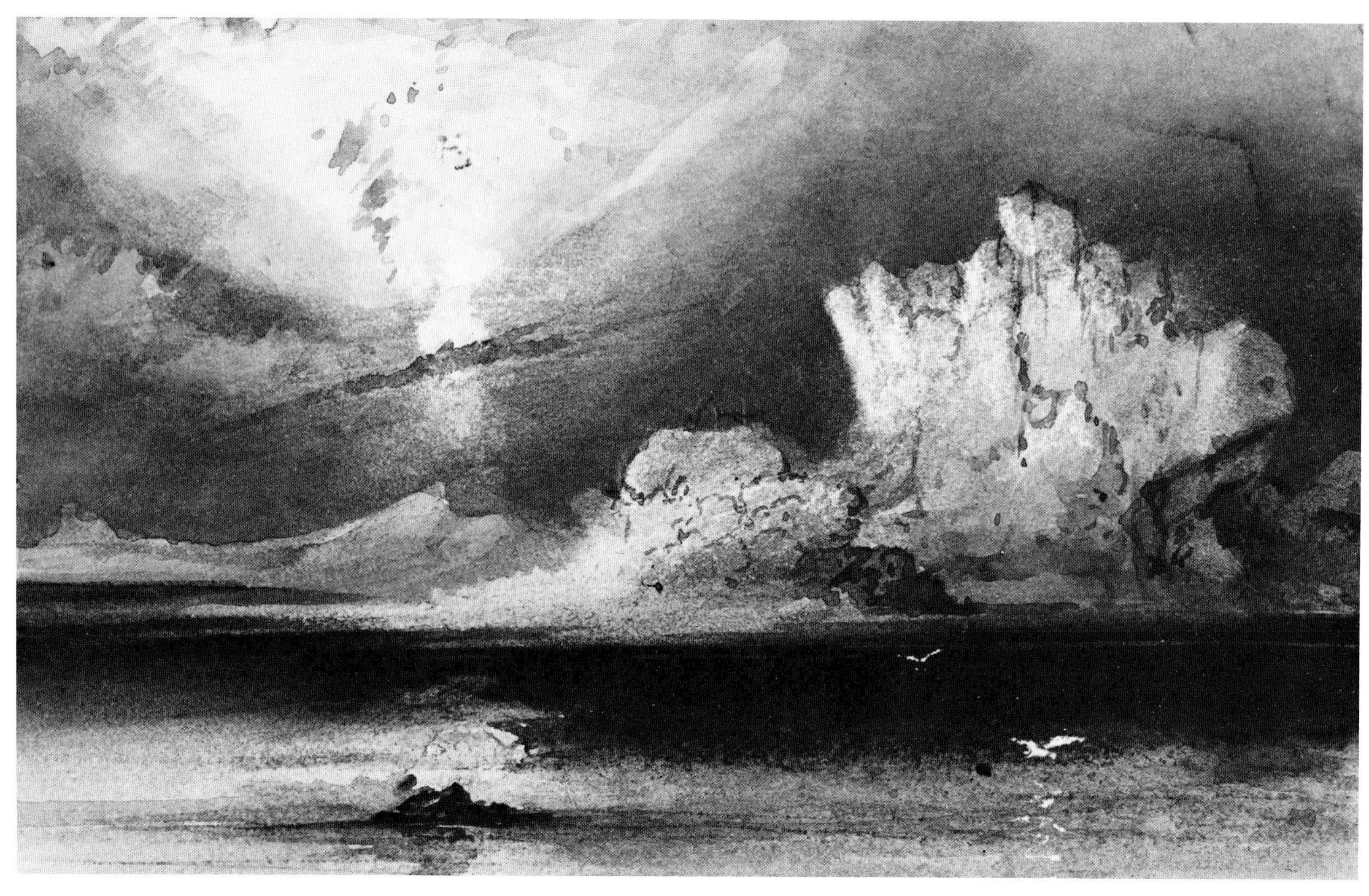

17. *Grounded Berg Near Cape York*, c.1853

Baffin's Bay,...There is a combination of warmth and cold in the tone of its landscapes, a daring, eccentric variety of forms, an intense clearness, almost energy of expression, which might tax Turner and Stanfield together to reproduce them with an approach to truth. How could they trace the features of the iceberg, melting into shapes so boldly marked, yet so defined; or body forth its cold varieties of unshaded white, or the azure clare-obscure of the ice-chasm!...All this attempered by the warm glazing of a tinted atmosphere. The sky of Baffin's Bay, though but eight hundred miles from the Polar limit of all northernness, is as warm as the Bay of Naples after a June rain. What artist, then, could give this mysterious union of warm atmosphere and cold landscape?" pp.148-149

Collection of Library Company, Philadelphia, Pa.

18. James Hamilton
(1819-1878)
Grounded Berg Near Cape York
c.1853
engraving
10.4 x 16.3 image
14.1 x 23.3 sheet
Recto: "Drawn by J. Hamilton from a Sketch by Dr. E.K. Kane, U.S. N. Engraved by J. Sartain"

Engraving by John Sartain in Elisha Kent Kane's *U.S. Grinnell Expedition*, (1854); facing p.144

Collection of Metropolitan Toronto Library.

19. James Hamilton
(1819-1878)
Entering Lancaster Sound, 1850
c.1852
ink wash and white highlights
10.7 x 18.2
Signed 1.1.: "J. Hamilton"

Provenance: Kane Family
Exhibition: *James Hamilton*, Brooklyn Museum, 1966
Appears to be the watercolour upon which John Sartain engraved the frontispiece to Kane's book *The U.S. Grinnell Expedition*, (1854).
Related to Chapter XX. August 19, 1850. "8 P.M. The breeze has freshened, to a gale. Fogs have closed round us, and we are driving ahead again, with look-outs on every side. We have no observation; but by estimate we must have got into Lancaster Sound." p.152

Collection of Mr. Gary Trinetti, Kane, Pa.   *Page 15

20. James Hamilton
(1819-1878)
Cape Riley, Erebus Bay, August 27, 1850
c.1852
watercolour over pencil
10.1 x 20.0
Verso: "Cape Riley Aug. 27, 1850 #28 Erebus Bay"

Provenance: Hilda France (N.J.)
            Kennedy Galleries, Inc., New York
Relates to Chapter XXI, *U.S. Grinnell Expedition*, (1854). Depicts the day the American and British explorers discovered Franklin's winter quarters, believing it would lead to finding the lost explorers. "On the 27th, the chances of this narrow and capricious navigation had gathered five of the searching vessels under three different commands, within the same quarter of a mile — Sir John Ross, Penny's and our own...I was still talking over our projects with Captain Penny, when a messenger was reported, making all speed to us over the ice...The news he brought was thrilling. 'Graves, Captain Penny! graves! Franklin's winter quarters!' We were instantly in motion... joined by a party from the 'Rescue', we hurried on over the ice, ...a weary walk, to the crest of the isthmus. Here, amid the sterile uniformity of snow and slate, were the headboards of three graves, made after the old orthodox fashion of gravestones at home." pp.161-162

Collection of Glenbow Museum
60.22.16   *Page 27

21. James Hamilton
(1819-1878)
Beechey Island Graves, 1850
c.1852
watercolour
16.6 x 27.9
Verso: "2022". Light pencil sketch of graves.

Provenance: Kane Family
See catalogue number 20.

Collection of Mrs. Florence Johnson, Mt. Jewitt, Pa. *Page 26

22. James Hamilton
(1819-1878)
Erebus Bay, Yellow Sunset
c.1850
watercolour
17.0 x 28.4

Provenance: Kane Family

Collection of Mrs. W. Beyer Africa, Warren, Pa.   *Page 24

23. James Hamilton
(1819-1878)
Wellington Channel, Beechey Island
c.1852
watercolour over pencil
9.5 x 30.1
Verso: "Wellington Channel, Beechey Island #30"

Provenance: Hilda France (N.J.)
            Kennedy Galleries, Inc., New York
Relates to Chapter XXV, *U.S. Grinnell Expedition*, (1854).
The Grinnell Expedition sailed north up Wellington Channel
Sept. 1855, hoping to penetrate into an open polar sea. Blocked
by ice, the explorers, before retreating, discovered new land
naming it after the expedition's patron, Henry Grinnell. "To
the large mass of land visible between northwest to north-
northeast, I gave the name of Grinnell, in honour of the head
and heart of the man in whose philanthropic mind originated
the idea of this expedition, and to whose munificence it owes its
existence," p.201

Collection of Glenbow Museum
60.22.21
                                         *Page 17

24. James Hamilton
(1819-1878)
Refraction
c.1852
watercolour
10.6 x 16.5
Verso: "Refraction #5"; pencil sketch of Beechey Island Graves
Provenance: Hilda France (N.J.)
            Kennedy Galleries, Inc., New York
Relates to Chapter XXVII, *U.S. Grinnell Expedition,* (1854).

Kane describes the apprehension felt as the expedition, caught
in the ice, drifted between Beechey Island and Leopold Island
towards Baffin Bay. The description refers to the explorer
witnessing refraction and the sighting of the graves on Beechey
Island. pp.234-235
See quote, catalogue number 25.

Collection of Glenbow Museum
60.22.25

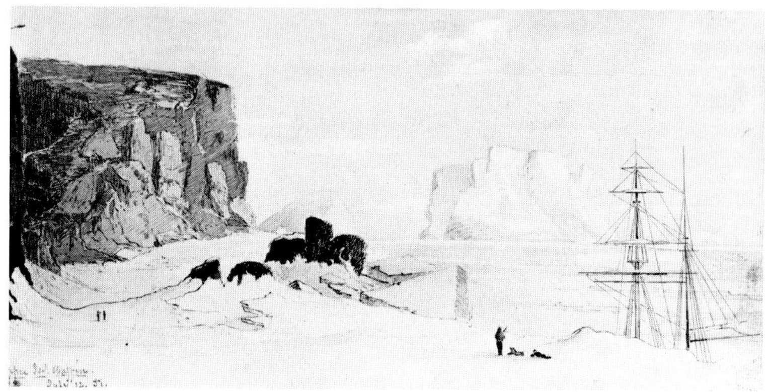

31. *Upper Island, Baffin, July 12, 1851,* 1851

25. James Hamilton
(1819-1878)
Leopold Island
c.1852
watercolour over pencil
10.0 x 27.0
Verso: "Leopold Island #16"

Provenance: Hilda France (N.J.)
            Kennedy Galleries, Inc., New York
Discussed in Chapter XXVIII, *U.S. Grinnell Expedition,*
(1854). "The month of November found us oscillating still with
the winds and currents in the neighborhood of Beechy Island.
Helpless as we were among the floating masses, we began to

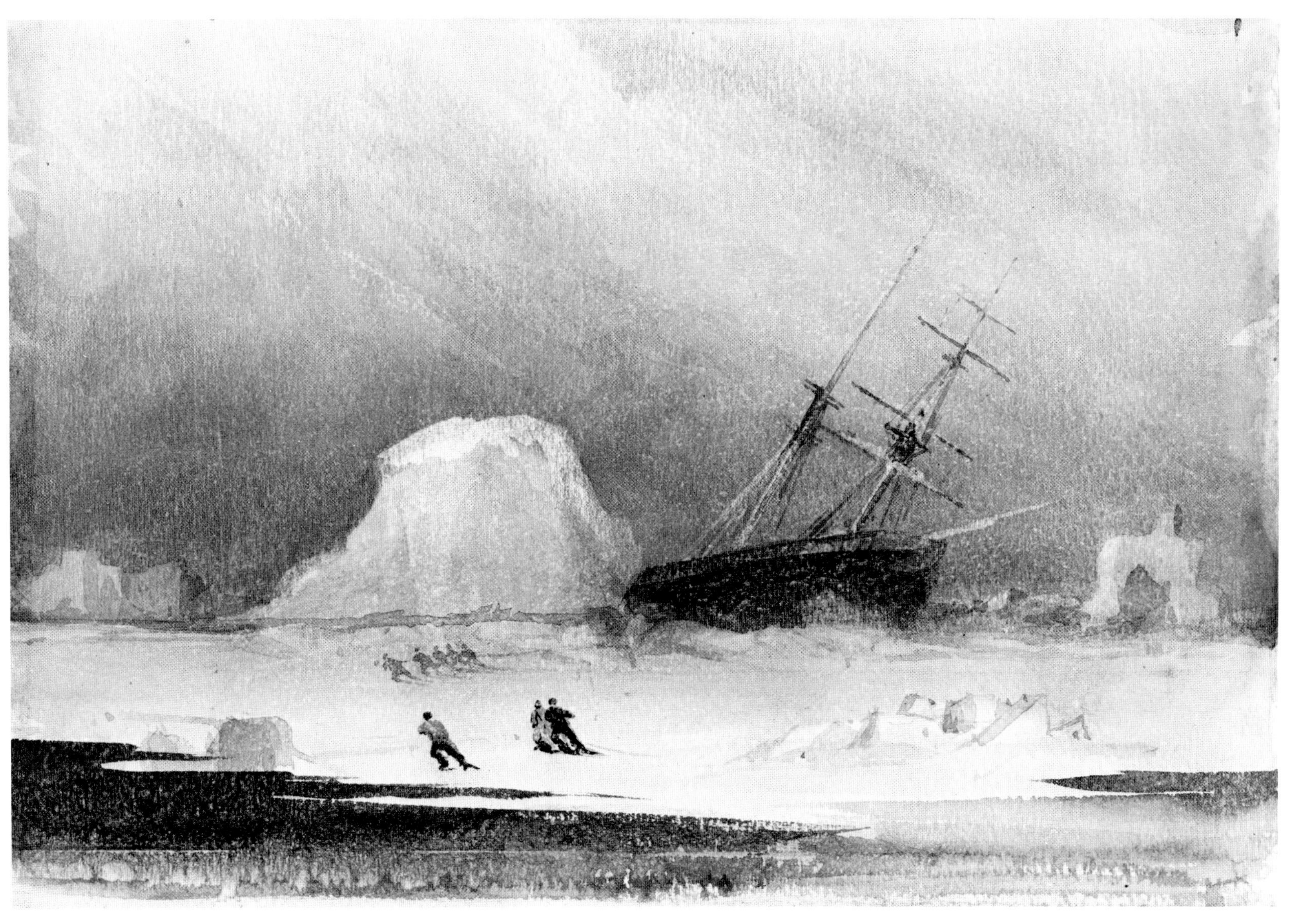

27. *Securing the Brig*, n.d.

look upon the floe that carried us as a protecting barrier against the approaches of others less friendly; and as the month advanced, and the chances increased of our passing into the sound, [Lancaster] our apprehensions of being frozen up in the heart of the ice-pack gave place to the opposite fear of a continuous drift. . . . At such times our floe would be deflected at an angle from its normal course, or would rotate slowly round its centre, and pass on — not, however, always in the same direction; sometimes nearing the western shore, sometimes closing in upon the beach of "the Graves" and sometimes fluctuating slowly to the northward. But our general course was toward the south and east. At daybreak on the 18th, Leopold's Island rose by refraction above the ice, standing with its unmistakable outline." pp. 234-235

Collection of Glenbow Museum
60.22.26

26. James Hamilton
(1819-1878)
'Rescue' In Her Arctic Ice Dock, 1851
c. 1852
watercolour
23.2 x 31.8

Provenance: Kane Family
Bibliography: Brooklyn Museum Exhibition Catalogue,
    James Hamilton, 1966 p. 15
Appears to be a study for an oil painting of the same title, catalogue number 28.
Inspired by a sketch of Elisha Kent Kane, and used for woodcut heading Chapter XXXVI of *U.S. Grinnell Expedition*, (1854), p. 324

Collection of Mr. Gary Trinetti, Kane, Pa.   *Page 23

27. James Hamilton
(1819-1878)
Securing the Brig
n.d.
watercolour
19.9 x 29.3
Verso: "For Mezzotint 2014"

Provenance: Kane Family

Collection of Mr. Gary Trinetti, Kane, Pa.   *Page 14

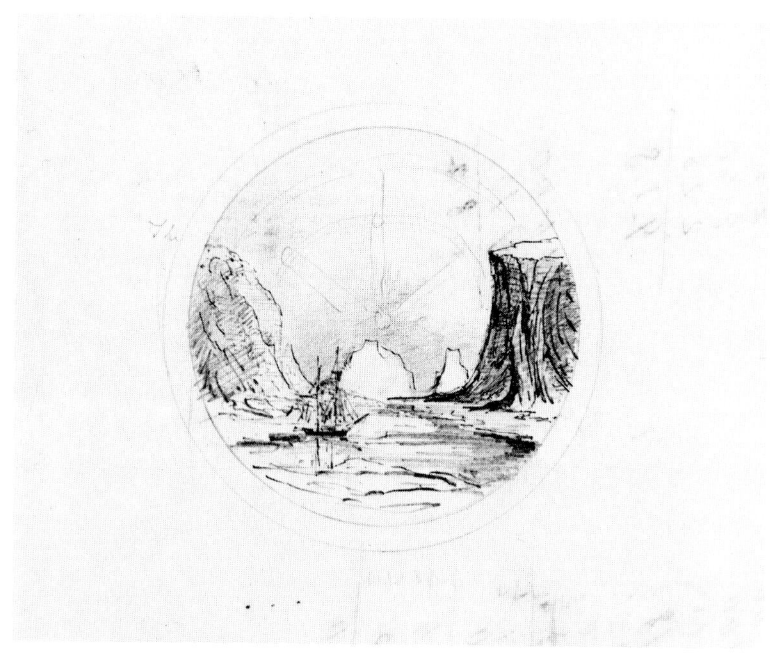

36. *Parhelina, Melville Bay*, c. 1851

28. James Hamilton
(1819-1878)
The 'Rescue' in Her Arctic Ice Dock
c. 1852
oil on canvas
91.2 x 74.2

Provenance: Grinnell Family
Exhibition: *James Hamilton,* Brooklyn Museum, 1966
Inspired by a sketch of Elisha Kent Kane (see Brooklyn Museum Catalogue, p. 15) and used for the woodcut heading Chapter XXXVI of *U.S. Grinnell Expedition*, (1854).
See also watercolour study catalogue number 26.
It depicts the explorers' ingenious method of creating a dry dock at latitude 72°, by cutting eight feet into the ice around the base of the ship providing an area enabling repairs to the keel. March, 1851. p. 324

Collection of Seneca Falls Historical Society, Seneca Falls, New York.   *Page 20

29. James Hamilton
(1819-1878)
Arctic Scene
n.d.
watercolour over pencil
17.6 x 26.3
Verso: "2010"

Provenance: Kane Family

Collection of Mrs. W. Beyer Africa, Warren, Pa.

30. James Hamilton
(1819-1878)
Arctic Scene
n.d.
watercolour over pencil
15.4 x 26.8
Verso: "2026"

Provenance: Kane Family

Collection of Mrs. W. Beyer Africa, Warren, Pa.

31. Elisha Kent Kane
(1820-1857)
Upper Island, Baffin, July 12, 1851
1851
watercolour, pencil and ink
12.2 x 24.7
Recto: b.1: "Upper lsl. Baffin, July 12.51."

Provenance: Kane Family
Though unsigned, the precisely delineated style is Kane's not
Hamilton's. Appears to be a direct study for woodcut *Scene at
Baffin's Islands,* p. 434.
Related to Chapter XLVII, *U.S. Grinnell Expedition,* (1854).
"The whalers call Baffin's Islands the Duck Islands, on account
of the number of these birds that breed there, and many of
their precipitous headlands Loonheads, for a similar reason. It
was fine sport for all hands to gather eggs from the rocky
crevices in which they build. The birds, when disturbed by our
predatory visits, literally darkened the air; and their quick,
sharp cries, the hum of their wings flapping around us, and the
surging noise of the sea as it broke against the base of their fortress below, all together might have startled a novice in the
trade of plunder. It was something like 'gathering samphire'."
pp. 433-434

Collection of Mr. Gary Trinetti, Kane, Pa.   *Page 14

32. James Hamilton
(1819-1878)
Greenland Fiord
n.d.
watercolour
10.5 x 16.7
Verso: "Greenland Fiord #20"

Provenance: Hilda France (N.J.)
            Kennedy Galleries, Inc., New York
Related to Chapter XLVIII, *U.S. Grinnell Expedition,* (1854)

Collection of Glenbow Museum
60.22.17   *Page 12

33. James Hamilton
(1819-1878)
Glacier from Near Upper Navik
c. 1852
watercolour
14.7 x 21.8
Verso: "Glacier from near Upper Navik #23"

Provenance: Hilda France (N.J.)
            Kennedy Galleries, Inc., New York
Related to Chapter XLVIII, *U.S. Grinnell Expedition,* (1854).
"As we travel...to the north, those great indentations known
as the Fiords, which penetrate the metamorphic ridges at right
angles to their long axes, serve as conduits to the interior ice...
the seats of large glaciers. These do not abut directly upon the
sea; but, as far as my inquiries extended, issue in troughs that
enter the fiords from the north and south, and are connected
with those great reservoirs, or *mers de glace*, which like vast
table lands, occupy the unknown interior." p. 447

Collection of Glenbow Museum
60.22.11

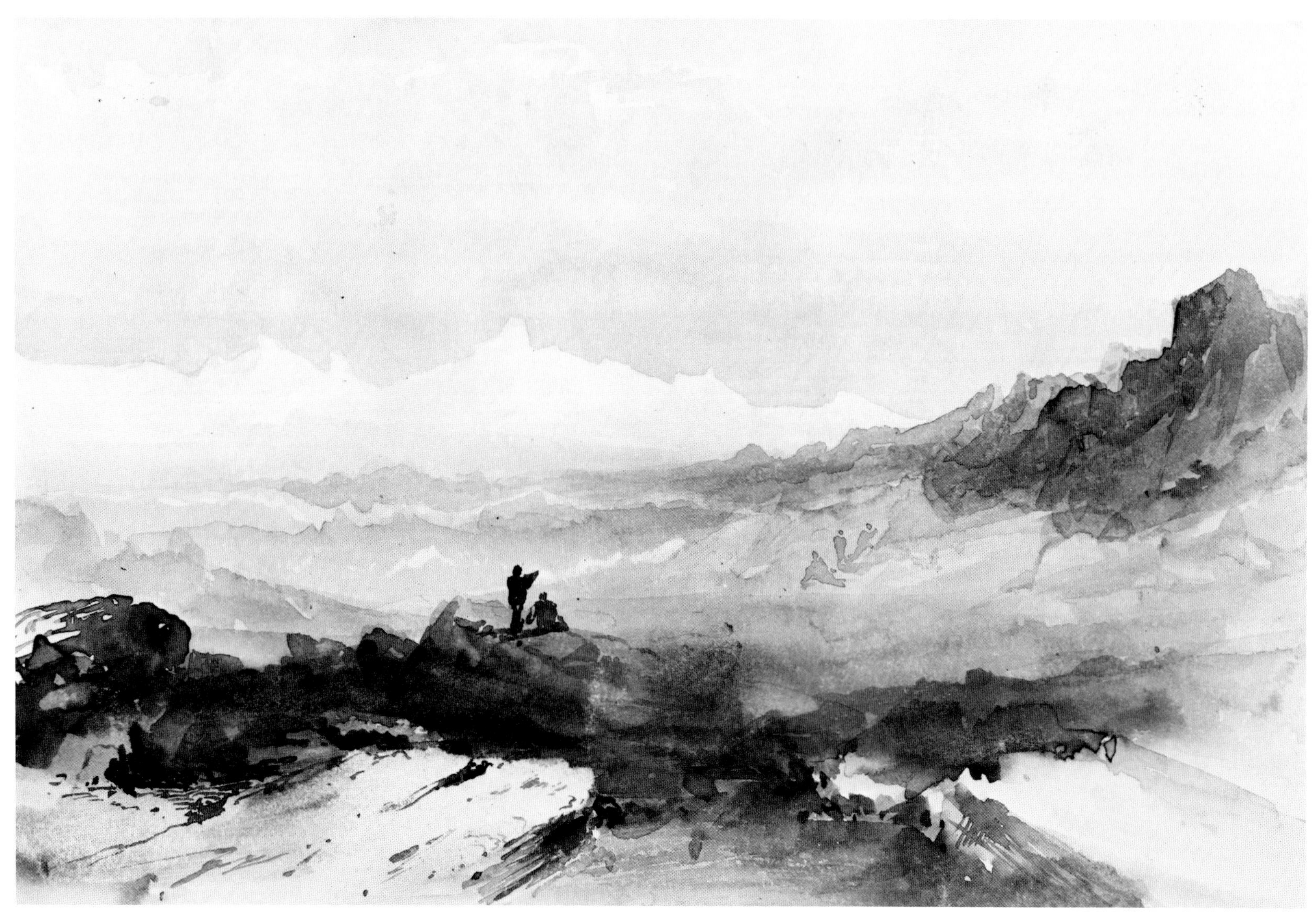

33. *Glacier from Near Upper Navik*, c.1852

34. James Hamilton
(1819-1878)
Greenland Fiord
n.d.
watercolour
16.0 x 24.3
Verso: "#2 Greenland Fiord"

Provenance: Hilda France (N.J.)
            Kennedy Galleries, Inc., New York

Collection of Glenbow Museum
60.22.24   *Page 16

35. James Hamilton
(1819-1878)
Breaking up of An Iceberg in Melville Bay
1852
oil on canvas
62.3 x 91.4
Signed I.I.: "J. Hamilton 1852"

Provenance: Kennedy Galleries, Inc., New York
            Bowdoin College, Maine
Exhibition: *James Hamilton*, Brooklyn Museum, 1966
Bibliography: The Kennedy Quarterly (bibl. 29, 1964)
Appears related to Chapter XLIX, "March and Collision of
Bergs...Berg Fractures," *U.S. Grinnel Expedition*, (1854).
"August 11, Monday [1851] We are still attached to the old
land-floe. This so-called land-ice is rather a huge field, hemm-
ed in by bergs, so as to be immovable. It is, however, young
and frail, not exceeding eighteen inches in thickness, and per-
forated with water-pools, cracks, and seal-holes. It is so rotten
that marginal pieces are continually breaking off, and carried
into the chaos of floating drift outside...As our protecting
floe gives way, therefore, men walk over the liberated tables
and plant our ice-hooks further off in the part that remains
solid.
August 17, Sunday "While profaining the day by an attempt to
sketch these sublime monuments of creative power in my drawing book, I was interrupted by a heavy undulation, rolling
under the brig, and passing on to the solid inshore floe...Up
to this moment all the heavy heaving and warping of to-day
had been without any effect. Now the floes separated as if by
magic: there was relaxation everywhere; and we made at least

two hundred yards before the ice closed again." pp. 464, 470

Collection of Mr. Ian McKibbon White, San Raffael,
Ca.   *Page 19

36. Elisha Kent Kane
(1820-1857)
Parhelina, Melville Bay
c. 1851
pencil and ink
10.7 diameter, image
18.5 x 19.7 sheet

Appears related to Chapter XLIX, *U.S. Grinnell Expedition*,
(1854) and woodcut page 463. "There were parhelina, intricate
ones, with six solar images and eccentric circles of light, one of
which had its circumference passing through the sun." p. 462

Collection of American Philosophical Society, Philadelphia,
Pa.

37. Elisha Kent Kane
(1820-1857)
Devil's Thumb
n.d.
watercolour and pencil
26.5 x 35.3
Recto: c.r. "Devil's Thumb."
Verso: "#6"
Provenance: Hilda France (N.J.)
            Kennedy Galleries, Inc., New York
The distinctive style of the small pencil sketch of the ship is that
of Elisha Kent Kane (see catalogue number 36). Devil's Thumb,
at the southern end of Melville Bay, was an important landmark for seamen. Discussed many times, including Chapter
XLVIII of *U.S. Grinnell Expedition*, (1854). "That singular
ejected rock, the Devil's Thumb, of which I have given several
sketches, stands in the recess of a curve of which Wilcox Point
forms a headland. The shore in its immediate neighbourhood is
not lofty but dotted here and there with hills jutting out
through massive glaciers. At the northern sweep of the indentation this ice-wall becomes more imposing; and in front of it we
found a progeny of bergs, crowded together so close that we
could not count them..." p. 445-446

Collection of Glenbow Museum
60.22.14

38. James Hamilton
(1819-1878)
The Open Water From Cape Jefferson
c.1856
engraving
9.8 x 17.2 image
22.4 x 13.6 sheet

Engraving by R. Hinshelwood from E.K. Kane's *Arctic Explorations* (Phila. 1856), Vol. I, facing p.307. Related to Chapter XXIII, describing the supposed discovery of the Open Polar Sea. "It must have been an imposing sight, as he stood at this termination of his journey, looking out upon the great waste of waters before him. Not a 'speck of ice' to use his own words, could be seen. There from a height of four hundred and eighty feet, which commanded a horizon of almost forty miles, his ears were gladdened with the novel music of dashing waves; and a surf breaking in among the rocks at his feet, stayed his farther progress." p.306

Collection of Glenbow Museum Library

39. Henry Collins Bispham
(1841-1882)
Dr. Kane in Search of Sir John Franklin, 1854
1865
oil
58.4 x 90.2 (sight)

Provenance: Kennedy Galleries, Inc., New York
Bispham exhibited at the Pennsylvania Academy 1861, '66, '68 with James Hamilton. Inspired by E.K. Kane's *Arctic Explorations* (1856).
Reproduced in Farley Mowat's *The Polar Passion: The Quest for the North Pole.* Toronto: McClelland & Stewart Ltd., 1967

Collection of Glenbow Museum
66.19.5

40. Elisha Kent Kane
(1820-1857)
Raising the Brig 'Advance'
c.1855
ink and pencil
10.5 x 18.4

Related to Chapter XXX, *Arctic Explorations*, (1856), Vol. I.
"We have been completing our arrangements for raising the brig. The heavy masses of ice that adhere to her in the winter make her condition dangerous at seasons of low tide. Her frame could not sustain the pressure of such a weight. Our object, therefore, has been to lift her mechanically above her line of flotation, and let her freeze in on a sort of ice-dock: so that the ice around her as it sinks may take the bottom and hold her clear of the danger. We have detached four of the massive beams that were intended to resist the lateral pressure of nips, and have placed them as shores, two on each side of the vessel, opposite the channels. Brooks has rigged a crab or capstan on the floe, and has passed the chain cable under the keel at four bearing-points. As these are hauled in by the crab and the vessel rises, the shores are made to take hold under heavy cleats spiked below the bulwarks, and in this manner to sustain her weight...
We made our first trial of the apparatus today. The chains held perfectly, and had raised the brig nearly three feet, when away went one of our chainslings, and she fell back of course to her more familiar bearings." p.401-402

Collection of American Philosophical Society, Philadelphia, Pa.

41. James Hamilton
(1819-1878)
Dudley Diggs, Baffin Bay
c.1855
watercolour over pencil
10.3 x 16.2
Signed 1.1.: "JH" [in monogram]
Verso: "Dudley Diggs Baffin #7"

Provenance: Hilda France (N.J.)
          Kennedy Galleries, Inc., New York
Relates to Chapter XXVII, *Arctic Explorations*, (1856) vol. II. The northern most end of Melville Bay, Dudley Diggs was a resting place for Dr. Kane and his men which they found before their final line of escape south to Upper Navik at the end of July, 1855. Kane named their camp site Providence Cliffs for its abundance of food and rugged comfort, writing of their stay as "...one glorious holiday." p.273

Collection of Glenbow Museum
60.22.22

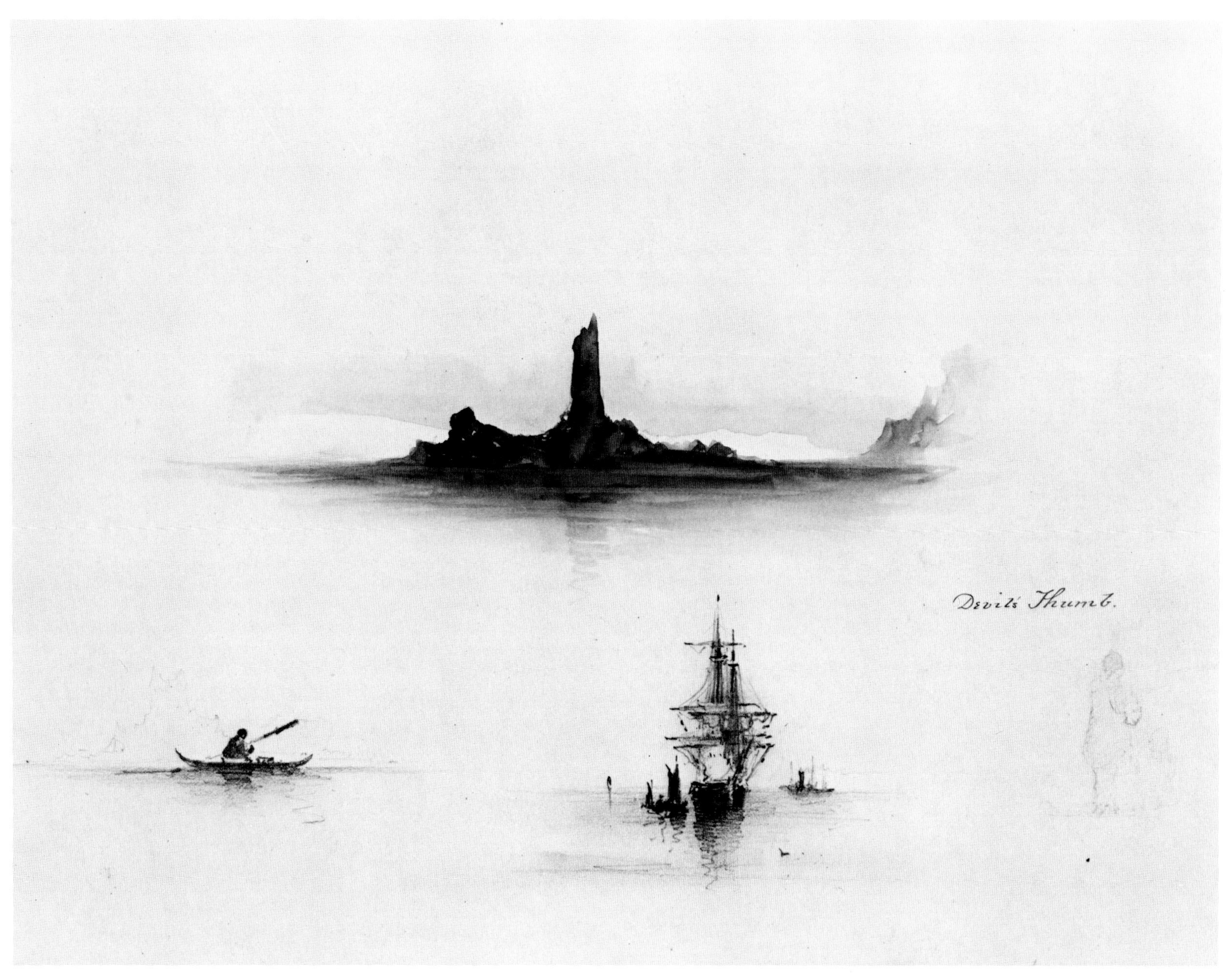

37. *Devil's Thumb*, n.d.

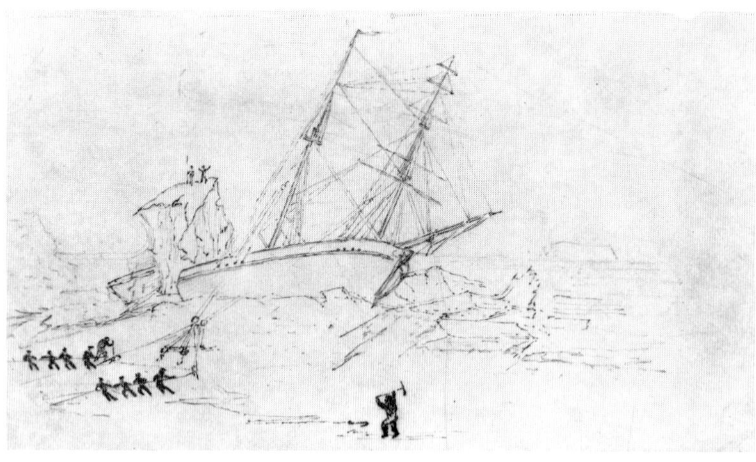

40. *Raising the Brig 'Advance'*, c. 1855

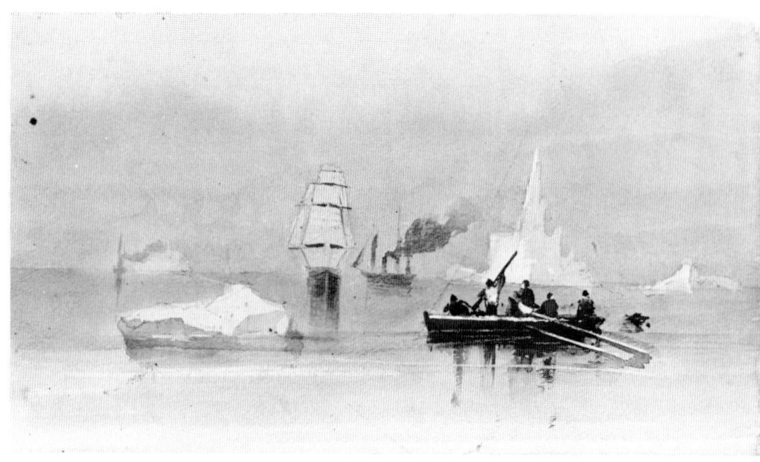

43. *Safe at Last*, c. 1855

42. James Hamilton
(1819-1878)
Steamer and Iceberg
c. 1856
watercolour over pencil
9.3 x 19.8
Verso: "Composition #26"

Provenance: Hilda France (N.J.)
             Kennedy Galleries, Inc., New York

Collection of Glenbow Museum
60.22.13

43. James Hamilton
(1819-1878)
Safe at Last
c. 1855
watercolour
19.2 x 32.2
Verso: "Same size 2030"

Provenance: Kane Family
Appears to relate to "Conclusion" of *Arctic Exploration*, (1856), Vol. II, Dr. Kane and members of his crew greeting the American squadron sent to their rescue on September 11, 1855.

"Presently we were alongside. An officer whom I shall ever remember as a cherished friend, Captain Harstene, hailed a little man in a ragged flannel shirt, 'Is that Dr. Kane?' and with the 'Yes.' that followed, the rigging was manned by our countrymen, and cheers welcomed us back to the social world of love which they represented." p. 297

Collection of Mr. Gary Trinetti, Kane, Pa.

The following works are among 43 drawings and watercolours contained in a folio, many signed by James Hamilton and Elisha Kent Kane. Originally understood to be a notebook, the collection was received too late to be considered in the essay. As they are of considerable interest, this selection has been included in the exhibition.

44. Elisha Kent Kane
(1820-1857)
The Rescue in her "ice dock"
c. 1851
pen and ink
20.5 x 31.5

Relates to Chapter XXXVI of *The U.S. Grinnell Expedition* (1854), p. 324, see catalogue numbers 26 and 28.

Collection of Dr. Thomas Kane.

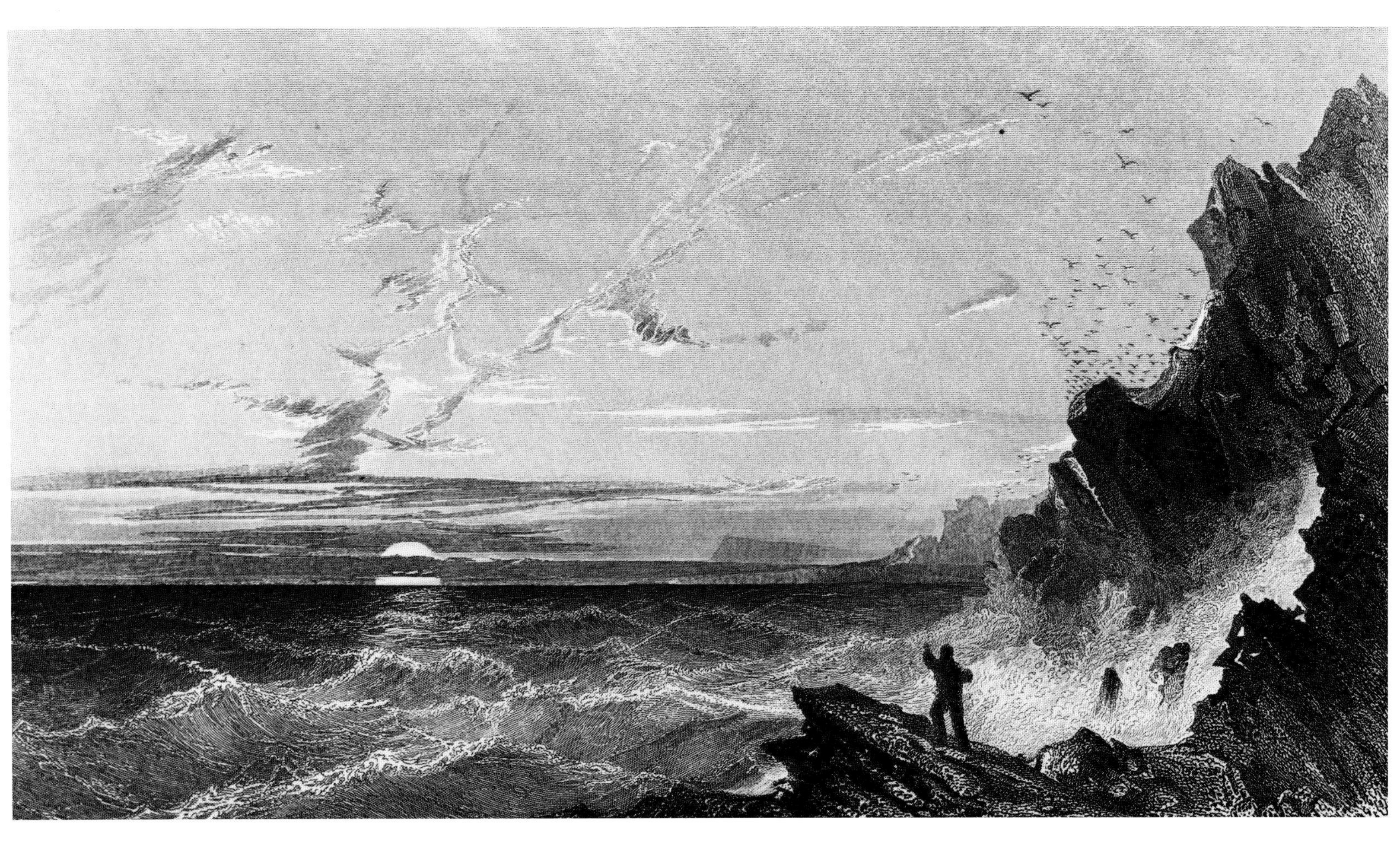

38. *The Open Water From Cape Jefferson*, c.1856

45. James Hamilton
(1819-1878)
Tennyson's Monument
c.1855
ink
18.0 x 9.2
Signed 1.1.: J. Hamilton

Bibliography: Charles W. Shields: "The Arctic Monument named for Tennyson by Dr. Kane." *The Century Magazine,* Vol. LVI, no.4, August 1898.

Image is a study for the engraving facing p.221.
"...in the immediate neighborhood of my haltinground beyond Sunny Gorge, to the north of latitude 79, a single cliff of greenstone, marked by the slaty limestone that once encased it, rears itself from a crumbled base of sandstones, like the boldly-chiselled rampart of an ancient city. At its northern extremity, on the brink of a deep ravine which has worn its way among the ruins, there stands a solitary column or minaret-tower, as sharply finished as if it had been cast for the Place Vendôme. Yet the length of the shaft alone is four hundred and eighty feet; and it rises on a plinth or pedestal itself two hundred and eighty feet high.
I remember well the emotions of my party as it first broke upon our view. Cold and sick as I was, I brought back a sketch of it, which may have interest for the reader, though it scarcely suggest the imposing dignity of this magnificent landmark. Those who are happily familiar with the writings of Tennyson, and have communed with his spirit in the solitudes of a wilderness, will apprehend the impulse that inscribed the scene with his name." p.224

Collection of Dr. Thomas Kane.

46. James Hamilton
(1819-1878)
The Open Water from Cape Jefferson
c.1855
ink
25.3 x 35.5 sheet
10.0 x 17.7 image
Signed l.l.: "J. Hamilton"
Recto l.r.: "Same subject on reverse side"
Verso: "Same subject on reverse side", ink drawing of same subject.

Relates to Chapter XXIII, *Arctic Explorations*, Vol. I, 1856.
See catalogue number 37.
Image is a study for the engraving facing page 307

Collection of Dr. Thomas Kane.

47. James Hamilton
(1819-1878)
The Bridge
c.1855
ink
16.3 x 22.8
Signed l.l.: "J. Hamilton"

Relates to Chapter XXVII, *Arctic Explorations,* Vol. II (1856).
The image is a study for the woodcut on page 271.
See catalogue number 41 *Dudley Diggs.*
"To soften the scene, a natural bridge opened on our right hand into a little valley cove, green with mosses, and beyond and above it, cold and white, the glacier." p.270

Collection of Dr. Thomas Kane.

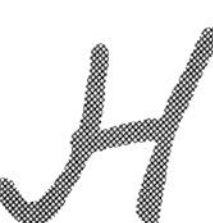

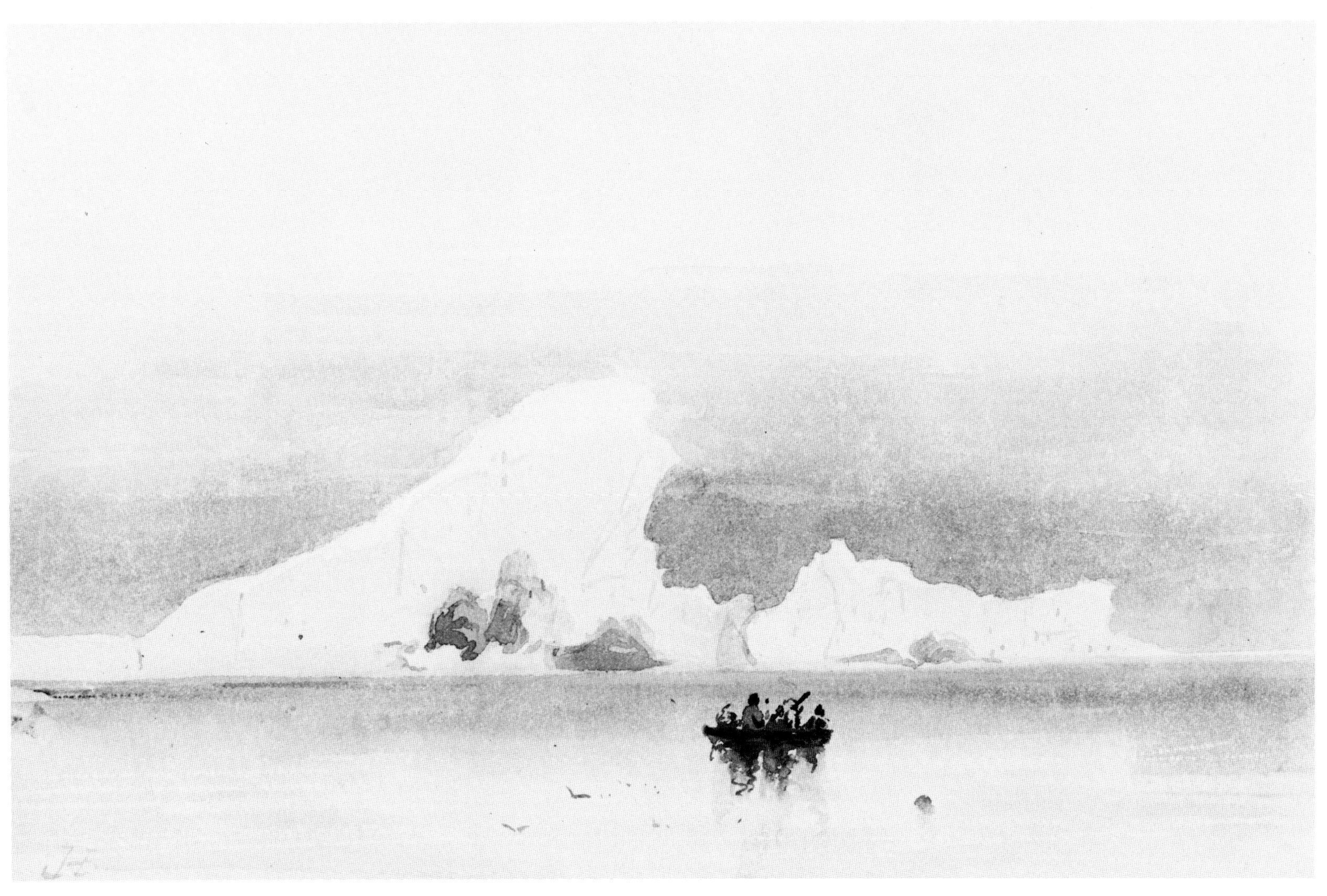

41. *Dudley Diggs, Baffin Bay*, c.1855

Lenders to the Exhibition

Mrs. W. Beyer Africa
Mrs. Robert Grinnell
Mrs. Florence Johnson
Dr. Thomas Kane
Mr. Gary Trinetti
Mr. Ian McKibbin White
Metropolitan Toronto Library
Seneca Falls Historical Society, New York
The American Philosophical Society, Philadelphia
The Library Company, Philadelphia

Design: Jane Poole
Photography: Kevin Oke
Typing: Marion DeVries
Editing: Jeremy Adamson, Donna Livingstone
Typesetting: Pamela Pountney
Printing: Hignell Printers, Winnipeg, Manitoba
© Glenbow-Alberta Institute, 1983
  130 - 9th Avenue S.E.
  Calgary, Alberta
  Canada, T2G 0P3